TIBET

THE ROOF OF THE WORLD
BETWEEN PAST AND PRESENT

WHITE STAR
PUBLISHERS

TIBET

THE ROOF OF THE WORLD
BETWEEN PAST AND PRESENT

Introduction
Kurt Diemberger

Texts by
Maria Antonia
Sironi Diemberger

Editorial coordination
Giulia Gaida

Graphic design
Luana Gobbo

Translation
C.T.M., Milan

Contents

© 2002, 2004 White Star S.r.l.
Via Candido Sassone, 22/24
13100 Vercelli, Italy
www.whitestar.it

ISBN 88-544-0010-6

REPRINTS:
 2 3 4 5 6 08 07 06 05 04

Printed in Korea

*1 The main entrance in a monastery marks
the passage between the world of the profane
and the world of the sacred and as such is
imbued with powerful symbolism.*

*2-3 This is Pang la Pass (16,800 feet),
the gateway to the valley of Everest.
From here, the Himalayan chain seems
very close beyond the pile of holy stones with
prayer flags.*

*4-5 The spiritual centre of Tibet is Jokhang
temple. This photograph was taken from the
temple's roof and shows the square, where
clouds of smoke rise from large braziers and*

crowds of pilgrims arrive every day from all over the world. The majestic Potala palace stands in the background.

6-7 Prayer flags, seen here hanging in the courtyard in front of Samye monastery, are one of Buddhism's most well-known symbols though they originated in the ancient cults of the mountain deities.

8 left This statue in Tashilumpo monastery is of Maitreya, the Buddha of the Future, one of the most common and widely worshipped images in Tibet.

8-9 Symbolic coloured festoons made from rectangular pieces of cloth are displayed on monastery roofs.
One of the most common interpretations of festoons is that yellow represents the earth, green water, red fire, white clouds and blue the sky.

8 right and 9 bottom Symbols found on monuments in Tibet are often made from gilded metal. Here we see a gyeltsen, a victory standard, and the Dharma wheel with gazelles, the symbol of the Buddhist religion.

10-11 The cham, the holy dance, is one of the most popular religious displays in Tibetan monasteries. This representation comes from Katok monastery in Kham which today is part of the province of Sichuan.

12-13 Among the traditional secular manifestations that have their roots in popular religious life, the horse race and archery competition are celebrated in honour of gods and heroes. This is a moment from the horse race at the festival of Gesar of Ling, the hero of the Tibetan epic, at Litang in Kham.

14-15 The north wall of Everest stands majestic and imminent above the meditation caves at the monastery of Rongbuk. Ascetics lived here in solitude for centuries in a setting that would take them to the limits of survival in winter. Abandoned during the Cultural Revolution, this place has, to a modest degree, recently been revitalised.

14 bottom Kurt Diemberger, seen here at over 23,000 feet above the Valley of Silence on Everest, reached the top of the highest mountain in the world in 1978, making the first film with synchronized sound of the climb at the same time. He returned to Everest in 1980 but bad weather forced him to halt on the South Col. In 1981 he was part of an American expedition that climbed the east wall; Diemberger's film of the ascent won the 1982-83 Emmy.

Introduction

by Kurt Diemberger

"**M**ake a quick visit to Tibet, just a quick visit..." This idea almost became an obsession as we moved among the gigantic ledges of snow that jutted out in every direction on the south crest of the Shartse. We were on the still virgin 23,000 foot mountain that forms the east peak of the Everest massif. We could only see a tiny part of a velley of Tibet, an almost hidden fragment, protected by the surrounding towering peaks. The strange buttresses of Makalu rose nearby, a 27,000 foot pyramid of reddish granite, no less impressive than Everest, which contrasted well with the white and blue of the contorted silhouettes on our crest.

Visit Tibet? Shartse was our main destination, of course, but it would certainly have been wonderful to at least enter the mysterious country, however briefly! There were a couple of white cols in front of us. Would it be possible to pass? What if there were precipices on the other side that would prevent access to the valley that called out to us more and more strongly with its magical voice? Would we find any people there? A shepherd maybe? We were able to see a glacier covered in drift, but in the distance there seemed to be some greenery. Probably there were alpine meadows further down. Maybe we could just dip down into the valley as the storms and wind whipped up a lacework of whirling snowflakes on the crest, making all progress impossible. Surely, we could at least have a look around and put our foot over the border into Tibet where we had never been before. And then, why not go further? At that time, in 1974, entry into Tibet was strictly forbidden, but who was there to see us? We felt that this was something to be decided when we were down there. When we arrived on the col some days later, the decision was taken out of our hands.

"Kurt, please don't hold me; let me down!" cried the imploring and desperate voice of my companion, Hermann, a German from Swabia, whom I could see gripping tightly onto the rope as he reared like a shying horse over the chasm. He wanted to rush down the steep slope. He was after his beloved Leica

which he had dropped, managed to skim with his hand but could not hold and now it was rolling unstoppable down towards Tibet. The Leica was his new, highly expensive camera, his pride and joy. The leather strap had broken and now flailed up and down like a tail of a mouse at play as the camera bounced down the mountainside.

I gritted my teeth and held on as immovable as an anchor, as rooted as a tree. Although Hermann covered me with the most colorful of German insults, I resisted him with all my strength. I did not want either of us to fall because of a single false move, which is so easy to do when hurrying down with crampons. Beneath us, the chasm dropped at least 1600 feet, perhaps even more since we could not see the base of the wall.

My friend had calmed down and was convinced he could find his Leica. "If we roll a few objects down, an empty gas bottle, or a tin of meat, perhaps they'll end up in the same place as the camera," said Hermann. Having launched some test objects, we descended by another col. The next day we entered the silent hidden valley. It was our first and unexpected encounter with Tibet, but we met no one. We spent the night in a bivouac between rocks and boulders and the next day tried to reach the base of the wall where we found the tin can and the gas bottle but no trace of the camera. "Perhaps a yeti's taken it," I joked but Hermann' s black look

15 top Shisha Pangma is detached from the Himalayan chain by Tong la Pass and extends north-west in the direction of the Brahmaputra river. Surrounded by barren land, it is the only mountain over 26,000 feet to stand completely in Tibetan territory.

15 bottom The hidden and deserted Karma chu valley has been a place of pilgrimage for centuries. Almost the ascetics of the modern world, mountain climbers on their way to the top of Everest have to overcome immense difficulties in polar cold temperatures. "Won't the mountain deities be offended?", Tibetans wonder as they try to understand such activities.

indicated how poorly it was taken. Yet this was truly a landscape for snow-men; a landscape with rugged boulders and the odd clump of grass, while on the other side of the valley, the mountains were gentler, rounded and coated with soft ice, like whipped cream. Further down, we could make out a splash of dark green that had to be the famous virgin forests of Kama chu which, I remembered, had been wonderfully described for the first time by the British in 1921. Under the leadership of George Mallory, they were searching for a way to the summit of Everest, but their on-the-spot investigation led them to conclude that the east wall was too dangerous. I took a few photographs of that interminable, spectacular wall not knowing one of them would open the door for my return to

Tibet seven years later with a large American expedition.

In the autumn of 1981, the Americans made the first attempt on the east wall of Everest, and I was the director of the expedition's documentary film. Naturally, the film included Lhasa, the Potala, and the majestic chain of Himalayan mountains seen from the north which I viewed from a pass at over 16,500 feet. I also filmed Shekar with its fort and monastery on the crystal-shaped mountain. I could not have known, of course, that in the winter of 1993 my daughter Hildegard, an anthropologist, Pasang Wangdu, a Tibetan historian, and I would make an interesting discovery in the monastery's library, a manuscript that was to prompt an important scientific paper. It was this manuscript that was to form the basis of the book, *The History of the White Crystal*, written by Hildegard and her mother, Maria Antonia Sironi.

Although I had visited some of the country's most famous places in 1981, the moment had not

yet arrived when Tibet was to be opened to me. As a mountaineer, I always had the mountains foremost in my mind: I did not know the language and if as a tourist, I thought I had understood the country after a ten-day trip, I had passed by the soul of Tibet and its people without even skimming it.

The first time I "felt" Tibet was in 1986 with a tribe of the mountain people who, centuries ago, left the plateau of Tibet to cross the high passes of the Himalayas and descended into the Makalu rain forests on the other side. I was fortunate enough to live for some months with these people while Julie, my companion on Nanga Parbat and K2, and I made a film about life in Tashigang, "a Tibetan village between the world of the gods and the world of men." It was a wonderful experience, both personally and professionally, and it was this that, thanks to my daughter, opened the doors of Tibet to me. I learned, for example, that the Naksong, the priest with the grey beard and bronze skin, was the title of the man who "had been in darkness", as the

16 top The ruins of Tholing are among the most important in the ancient kingdom of Guge in western Tibet. This is where Atisha, the great Indian master supported by the local lords, succeeded in rekindling Buddhism in Tibet in the 11th century.

16 bottom The second of the Guge capitals was Tsaparang which was also a great spiritual centre. Reduced to a mass of ruins, traces of wonderful paintings can still be found among the remains of some buildings.

16-17 *Gurla Mandhata is a mighty 23,000 foot mountain that overlooks Lake Manosarovar. In the twilight, the monastery of Chiu, an obligatory stop on the* khora *around the lake, can be seen on the right.*

17 top *Some* stupa *and broken down sections of wall are all that remain of the monastic complex of Tholing. Built at the start of the 11th century on the Indian model of the* mandala, *it became the largest monastery in western Tibet with magnificent paintings in what is known as "Guge style".*

17 bottom *Above Lake Manosarovar, the monastery of Chiu awakes as the first rays of the sun illuminate the east wall of Mount Kailash. The monastery stands where tradition says that Padmasambhava spent the last seven days of his earthly life.*

word *nak* means forest as well as black, i.e., "what is in shadow." The Naksong is in contact with the forces of nature, with the spirits that live in the rocks, the trees and the waters. It is his duty to placate them, to make them offerings, and to purify the impure. He also acts as a healer using medicinal herbs, but most importantly, his task is to cure the true roots of evil. He represents the oldest form of pre-Buddhist religion in the mountains and performs his functions with the Lama, a member of the Nyingmapa sect, the oldest form of Tibetan Buddhism. The two celebrate together during rituals, weddings and pilgrimages to the holy places. Accustomed to disputes that have their roots in religious matters throughout the rest of the world, I was struck by the peaceful collaboration between the Naksong and the Lama at Tashigang.

Years later, I found myself once more in Tibet with Hildegard, this time before the tombs of the kings in the valley of Chonggye. Here I came to know figures from Tibetan legends and then, bit by

18-19 The satellite photograph shows clearly the branches of the Yamdrok tsho, the "lake in the shape of a scorpion", that push their way into the deep valleys. The Yamdrok tsho is considered by Tibetans to be one of the great holy lakes. The course of the Brahmaputra can be seen at the top left with the Kyichu tributary, the river on which Lhasa was built.

19 top Satellite photographs taken during the last few years give a unique view of the Himalayas and surrounding terrain. The white pyramid of Everest can be seen in the centre with its north slope in shadow.

19 centre The Himalayan chain seen from a satellite showing Lake Manosarovar and Gurla Mandata (top left). Smudges of smoke can be seen on the southern and greener side of the chain compared to the northern desert lands. The smoke is the result of the "slash and burn" technique periodically used by inhabitants of the southern slopes of the Himayalas to free portions of forest for cultivation.

19 bottom The large snow-capped mountains of Karakorum and Ladakh stand on the border between Kashmir and Tibet. The picture shows the thick furrow of lakes that stretches from Dyab co in Tibet to Pangong in Kashmir. Their waters run into the river Indus.

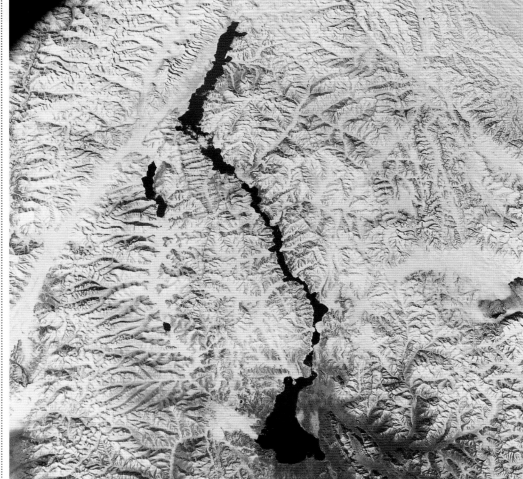

20 top and bottom The golden roofs of the Jokhang are rich with symbolic decorations: the symbol of Buddhism shows two gazelles, representing Buddha's first sermon to his disciples in the garden of the gazelles at Sarnath, and an eight-spoked wheel, the Dharma wheel.

20 centre Simple and modest in everyday life, the monks dress elegantly in their ceremonial clothes on grand occasions. Here we see a young monk wearing a typical in Xiasa monastery in east Tibet.

bit, the histories of the Tibetan kings themselves. I can add with satisfaction that discovery is not the exclusive privilege of the experts. High up in the castle of Yumbu Lagang, I wondered what the mountain of Yarlha Shampo must be like. I heard that this was where the mythical kings arrived on earth after their descent from heaven. The guides spoke of a "small hill," perhaps just 16,500 feet high, at the bottom of the Yarlung valley and the experts seemed disposed to accept this version. My mountaineering spirit was aroused and I felt I simply had to find this mountain.

I managed to hire a jeep and set off up the valley along roads which got progressively worse. After an infinite series of fords, interruptions, and deviations through the fields, it appeared in front of me: large, splendid, and covered with a brilliant white hood of snow, Yarlha Shampo, a mountain worthy of the gods and a god itself. It was at least 19,500 feet high and probably not easy to climb. At the base, in a small monastery, I also found the *thangka* of the white yak, the animal image of the god Yarlha Shampo.

20-21 Yumbu Lagang is the castle built by Tibetan kings on a spur that dominates the Yarlung valley. From this "cradle of the Tibetan civilization", they governed the country with wisdom and good judgement before moving the capital to what was to become Lhasa. Destroyed in the Cultural Revolution, the ancient castle has since been faithfully reproduced.

Since then, Tibet and its history have continued to appear evermore profound even to my eyes, and now I understand that this country is a crystal of many facets that always shines with new and intense light from whatever direction you look at it. Each manuscript that gets translated is a tile in a mosaic and each interview is a shaft of light that contributes to the illumination of new corners of the country and its history. Now I understand why Hildegard and Maria Antonia visit that distant land each year, enamoured by its infinite number of crystal facets.

As President of a volunteer association that builds schools and health facilities in Tibet, Maria Antonia has travelled around the Roof of the World for years to check on works in progress. She is continuously collecting anecdotes, stories, and pictures of the country and learning about the difficulties experienced by the people she meets. Her experiences in Tibet have provided the basis for this introduction to the country, its present and its past. Supported by splendid photographs, it has been written for those who wish to look beyond the old and the new myths of Tibet into the kaleidoscope of images that coexist in the daily life of the Land of Snows.

21 top left A Buddha painted on a rock overlooking a small lake on the road to Lhasa has been a landmark for pilgrims on their way to the capital for centuries.

21 top right In life as in their modes of dress, Tibetan women combine tradition with products that have been available in markets for some years, like modern windcheaters.

22-23 Common prayers are a fundamental element in monastery life. Here at Sakya, the monks assemble and remain almost immobile for hours at a time. In the freezing temperatures of the temple where there is no means of heating, the monks try to keep warm by wearing thick woollen cloaks.

Tibet between myth and history

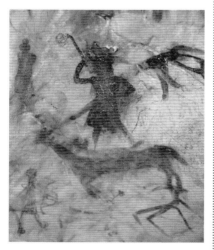

24 top right The tombs of the kings belong to the first chapter of the history of Tibet when the kings became mortal beings. The royal tumuli are located at Chonggye in the Yarlung valley that is considered their ancestral home.

24 top left The histories of the Tibetan kings are recounted in the manuscripts found in the Dunhuang oasis. These documents allow the myths and stories that accompanied the birth of the kingdom of Tibet to be reconstructed.

"Fifty thousand years for the scrapers". This is the age calculated by Chinese researchers of the oldest human traces in Tibet, at Dingri, a fluvial terrace at 14,000 feet, which they have ascribed to the Middle or Late Palaeolithic period. Remains found in eastern central Tibet, on the other hand, are considered to date from the Neolithic period. Examples of graffiti in remote areas, particularly in the north, still await the expert eye and the infinite patience of scholars.

It is thought that Tibetans are descended from several nomadic tribes that migrated south-west from the steppes of central-eastern Asia to mix with existing and unknown peoples. As the centuries passed, these tribes moved down the Brahmaputra basin where they learnt to work the soil, settled and gave rise to the Tibetan civilization. The origin of the highland nomads is more obscure: the little we know has reached us from brief mentions in Chinese and Tibetan sources and from later documents relating to the Bonpo religion. These have brought us knowledge of the existence of the kingdom of Shang Shung, of its probable capital at Kyunglung Ngulkar on the river Sutlej, and the fact that it was very large even if its size was not defined. Some experts think that this people was able to extract the mineral resources — perhaps gold — which abound beneath the subsurface.

Among the more reliable sources with a bearing on Tibetan history are the Dunhuang documents, an impressive pile of papers that remained buried in a cave in the Dunhuang oasis for at least a thousand years before they were found in miraculously good condition by Paul Pelliot and Sir Aurel Stein at the beginning of the 20th century. They contain documents, annals, accounts and ritual texts from various epochs that have provided scholars with abundant information on the Tibetan empire. The kingdom of Shang Shung is also named in the Dunhuang documents as having been conquered by the great Tibetan king, Songtsen Gampo. A song cycle narrates the events

24 bottom left Petroglyphs indicating traces of ancient civilizations have been found in various parts of the country. This one comes from Shensa in the province of Nagchu.

24 bottom right The Jokhang, shown in this picture of 1290, is one of the oldest buildings constructed by the Tibetan civilization and was built by Songtsen Gampo when he moved his capital to Lhasa. Over the centuries, its image has been reproduced on thangka and in frescoes so that we are able to study its architectural development.

25 Songtsen Gampo, whose image is shown here in an important statue that stands in the Potala, was the first Tibetan king to whom a historical date can be assigned: he died in 649 AD. He massively expanded the Tibetan kingdom, moved the capital to Lhasa and is considered the person that introduced Buddhism to Tibet. This last fact is symbolised by the small Buddha's head seen in his hat.

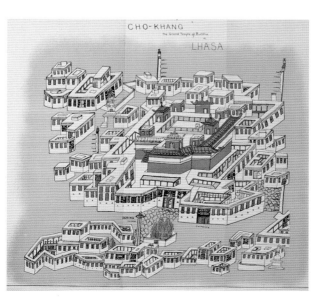

26-27 Samye, the first Buddhist monastery in Tibet, was built and inaugurated by king Trisong Detsen in 779. Its construction is depicted in this ancient fresco carefully preserved in the small apartment of the Dalai Lama on the second floor of the monastery.

26 bottom This fresco describes the meeting between king Trisong Detsen and Padmasambhava that occurred on the road to Samye. The chronicles tell us that the king arrived with great pomp and only prostrated himself before Padmasambhava when he recognised the master's magic powers. The small chorten on the right were erected to commemorate the great event.

in the life of the Tibetan princess, sister of Songtsen Gampo, who was given to the king of Shang Shung to be his wife. In his commentary on the song cycle, Gesa Uray, one of the most knowledgeable scholars of the history of ancient Tibet, recounts that the girl reached her intended husband in his far-off land but that the marriage was not consummated. When Songtsen Gampo came to hear of it, he was disappointed and considered his sister to be responsible. He immediately ordered her to perform her marital duty as it was her task to give birth to a son, but the responsibility actually lay with her husband who refused to have an heir that would put him in a position of vassalage to the king of Tibet. The princess was offended and turned to her brother for help. She sent him an allegorical message – the song cycle – in which she revealed the true situation of the country; she described the ranks of the nobility as being disloyal to the king and invoked military intervention. In reply, Songtsen Gampo sent an army and in 644-645 he conquered the kingdom of Shang Shung.

Songtsen Gampo was a great general and the ruler of a country where Buddhism was just gaining a foothold, although later chronicles celebrate him as a champion of the new religion. He was one of the first historically documented kings in a history

as the Taklimakan desert and the famous Khotan oasis, where the Silk Road passed. The Tibetan king created family links with China by marrying the emperor's daughter, Wengchen, and with Nepal by marrying the king's daughter, Bhirikuti, though the historical authenticity of this second wife is still debatable. Tradition tells us that these two wives brought refined elements from their cultures into the coarse Tibetan court and, most important, introduced the seeds of Buddhism. Songtsen Gampo is famous as the king who proclaimed the first written law and transferred the capital to Lhasa where he built Buddhism's largest temple, the Jokhang.

In 755, Trisong Detsen ascended the throne of Tibet. This king strengthened the kingdom and in 763 managed to penetrate, if only for 15 days, Ch'ang-an, the capital of the Chinese empire during the Tang dynasty, near the present day Xian. Considered the great diffuser of Buddhism in Tibet, Trisong Detsen's childhood and early reign were marked by conflict between the followers of the new religion and those faithful to the autochthonous gods which were later to be called "Bonpo". These years were a period of intrigue and cunning on both sides and are described in the accounts of the construction of the monastery of Samye. When the king was still young and Masham, his uncle-cum-minister who acted as regent, persecuted the followers of Buddhism, bad omens appeared; the country was struck by natural disasters and terrible misfortunes afflicted the regent's closest allies:

" ... the minister Tanglabar was led to the feet of Thang lha mountain where he died screaming for a long time "kwa kwa", the minister Chogro Kyesan Gyalgong died by having his tongue and legs dried out. As for the uncle-cum-minister, Masham, after great omens of death appeared, female diviners declared, following payment by his enemies, that "the divination for the king is very inauspicious". Consequently, the uncle-cum-minister was sent to be buried alive as a ransom".

But Buddhism was not completely victorious even then. The Bonpo attributed the natural disasters to the introduction of the new religion and forced Shantarakshita, the Indian master who taught Buddhism at court, to leave. A debate between the Bonpo and the Buddhists was held to resolve the issue and the new doctrine won. The king started construction of the first Buddhist monastery at Samye on the left bank of the Brahmaputra for which he brought back Shantarakshita from India accompanied by Padmasambhava, the magus-master of Tantrism who was the only person able to definitively subdue the local spirits opposed to Buddhism. Tibetan tradition says that every night these spirits destroyed what had been built during the day until Padmasambhava succeeded in taming them with the force of his magic, turning them into defenders

that becomes increasingly blurred by myth as it retreats into the past. Tradition has it that the kings of Tibet were descended from the gods: at the beginning of his earthly life, the king descended from heaven on a cord of light. He touched the earth on a sacred mountain and governed his subjects with wisdom. At the end of his task, he ascended to heaven once more via the cord of light that had never left him. One day, the seventh or eighth king of Tibet whirled his sword over his head while fighting and accidentally cut the cord of light. Having severed his link with the divine, the king fell dead, mortal amongst mortals. Since then, it has been necessary to perform funeral ceremonies for each dead king and place his body in a tomb. The Chonggye valley was chosen as a burial site where the many tumuli are impressive memorials to past pomp and glory.

Myth turned to history during the 6th century. The grandfather and father of Songtsen Gampo, the conqueror of Shang Shung, are referred to in the documents. As great soldiers and able strategists, they enlarged and consolidated the kingdom of Tibet. When Songtsen Gampo ascended the throne, he put down the warrior chiefs and tribes behind the Nyenchen Tanglha mountain chain, passed through the conquered Shang Shung kingdom, crossed the Kunlun mountains and continued as far

27 top Stelae, known as doring, are valuable historical documents as their information, cut in stone, is almost ineradicable. One of the most well-known is the stele at Samye that gives the text of Trisong Detsen's edict of 779 that proclaimed Buddhism as the state religion.

27 centre A famous stele in front of the Jokhang contains the text of the pact signed in 821-22 between the king of Tibet and the Emperor of China which proclaims respect of the borders between the two countries and a reciprocal agreement of non-aggression. The stele also calls on all the gods and all men to witness the agreement.

27 bottom right The oldest of the three stelae stands in front of the Potala. It records the victory of the Tibetan king Trisong Detsen over the Chinese in 763 when he entered their territory with his large army and took the capital of the Chinese empire, Ch'ang-an, if only for 15 days. During the Tang dynasty, this city was located near the present-day city of Xian.

27 bottom left This image shows a fresco, situated in Samye monastery, representing a part of the monastery itself.

of the new religion. Samye was inaugurated in 779 and has been the spiritual centre of Buddhism in Tibet ever since. The first monks were ordained at Samye and Trisong Detsen proclaimed a famous edict in which he recognised Buddhism as the state religion but, slowly, new doctrinal conflicts arose within the new faith between followers of the Chinese and Indian schools of Buddhist thought.

The religion spread with the descendants of Trisong Detsen. The number of monasteries increased and translation of holy texts from Sanskrit and Chinese into Tibetan flourished. In 821-822, a pact of non-aggression was signed between China and Tibet: the text was written in both the Chinese and Tibetan languages on the stele in front of the Jokhang in 823. Its content ran as follows:

... the great ruler of Tibet and the great ruler of China, respectively nephew and uncle, met and signed an agreement for a system of common government and stipulated a great peace. All gods and men were called to witness the treaty... The two countries, Tibet and China, must each protect their land and borders. All that is to the east of that border is the land of the great China, all that is to the west is the land of the great Tibet. The two parties shall not fight as enemies nor lead warring armies nor invade each other's territories.

The signing of the agreements and their related oaths were accompanied by animal sacrifices within the context of pre-Buddhist and Chinese ceremonies.

The defenders of the local deities were far from being crushed however. Belonging to large and powerful families, they saw serious danger to the state in the expansion of the new faith and monastic communities and they set to work to defend it. One such person was prince Langdarma who ferociously persecuted the Buddhist monastic institutions once he became king. The communities were deprived of their assets and the monks driven out until, to prevent the king from adding to his sins, a monk decided to assassinate him – which he did consummately in 842.

The assassination was followed by years of darkness during which the kingdom of Tibet disintegrated. A few monks journeyed eastwards "to

keep the spark of religion alive" but then "the flame was rekindled in the west". Some descendants of the royal family migrated west where they created the small kingdoms of west Tibet that adopted a philo-Buddhist policy. They called on craftsmen and painters to build large works such as the temple of Tholing and they encouraged the diffusion of holy texts by inviting illustrious teachers and translators like Atisha who arrived from India in 1042. Most of the masters came from Swat, Kashmir and west India where the expansion of Islam was persuading philosophers and thinkers to cross into Tibet. The first centuries of the second millennium also brought masters, translators and Tibetan ascetics – including Marpa and Milarepa – who helped Buddhism to flourish once more.

At the start of the 13th century, a new danger cast its shadow over Tibet. Under the leadership of Genghis Khan, the Mongols had developed into an unstoppable force intent on conquering all of central Asia. In 1210 they attacked Peking, burned down the city, slaughtered the inhabitants and instated their own capital under the Yuan dynasty which ruled China until 1368. Yet, when he came to Tibet, after a breaf invasion Genghis Khan halted: the reason, Tibetan tradition tells us, is that he was interested in Buddhism and the teachings of the great masters. True or false, Tibet was saved, in fact an agreement was signed between the Great Khan, the emperor of China, and the monks of Sakya monastery in south-west Tibet. Invited to the court in Peking, the Lamas of Sakya were appointed spiritual guides in return for a sort of vassalage which guaranteed the emperor political patronage over Tibet. The Sakya-*ponchen*, the abbot of Sakya monastery, became the governor of a unified country; he reorganised its administration on a Mongol model and even created a postal service.

From the middle of the 13th century, leadership

28 top *Tsongkhapa (1357-1419), one of the fundamental figures in Tibetan history, was the great reformer of Buddhism and the founder of the Gelugpa sect. The coming to power of the Gelugpa signalled the start of the theocratic state with the Dalai Lama at its head and was to last until the middle of the 20th century.*

28 bottom *Genghis Khan was the great and terrible Mongol warlord that created the Khan empire. In 1239-40 he briefly invaded Tibet but – Tibetan sources insist – the wonders of the country convinced him to withdraw his troops and establish a relationship with the monks and lords of Sakya based on patronage. The consequence of this development was that rulers of Sakya governed Tibet for roughly a century with the support of the Khan.*

29 top *Genghis Khan and his successors were fiery, implacable warlords whose notoriety spread across all the known world. The Mongol hordes succeeded in conquering vast tracts of central Asia and made Peking their capital. The picture shows them in battle against the Chinese in a 1397 painting by an artist from Shiraz.*

29 centre *Milarepa lived in western Tibet during the 11th and 12th centuries. He was one of the great masters that brought about the rebirth of Buddhism after the dark centuries that followed the collapse of the Tibetan empire. Poet, mystic and magician, he had a great number of disciples who founded the Kagyupa sect with Milarepa as its "patron saint".*

29 bottom right *The fifth Dalai Lama (1617-1682) was one the greatest figures in Tibetan history. He brought the Gelugpa sect to power and with the help of the Mongols restored the kingdom to its ancient magnificence. To crown his glory, he built the Potala palace in which his remains are still kept.*

of the country passed amongst several families associated with different religious sects but below them the local nobles continued to conduct their personal wars, changes of alliances, marriages and betrayals. Within this context, religious works became an expression and the legitimisation of the power of the nobles who sponsored them. This was how all the texts of the Buddhist canon, translated and commented upon by the great masters, came to be collected in the monastery of Narthang in central-western Tibet in the first half of the 14th century. From this followed the immense work called Kanjur and Tenjur – the set of texts that respectively report the word of Buddha and its commentaries – that forms Tibetan Buddhism's equivalent of the Bible. Meanwhile, a class of highly capable Tibetan Buddhist masters had been created whose teachings ranged across every field of human knowledge. This was the age of great figures like Tsongkhapa, the founder of the Gelugpa sect, or Bodong Chole Namgyal, distinguished writer and founder of the Bodongpa tradition. The last of the families to guide the country was that of the kings of Tsang, who had their seat at Shigatse. They governed until 1642 when they were defeated by the troops of a Mongol tribe called to aid the fifth Dalai Lama.

The title Dalai Lama is of Mongol origin and means "ocean". The first man to be conferred the title was an abbot of the Gelugpa sect who received it in 1575 from Altan Khan, the leader of the dominant Mongol clan, but the abbot was only considered to be the third Dalai Lama with the name of Sonam Gyatso as two dead disciples of Tsongkhapa were awarded the title posthumously. The fourth Dalai Lama, on the other hand, was worshipped as the reincarnation of Altan Khan. As

soon as the fifth Dalai Lama had ascended the throne, he called on the Mongols to help him defeat the king of Tsang; in return the title of king of Tibet was conferred on their leader but the Dalai Lama retained power in his own hands. He sanctioned the rise of the Gelugpa sect and, to seal his own position, moved his seat to Lhasa where he commenced the construction of the palace of Potala on the red hill that dominates the city.

Meanwhile a new force, the Manchu, was emerging in China. They reached Peking in 1644 where they imposed the Qing dynasty. In Tibet there followed a period of struggles, disputes and wrangling between Tibetans, Chinese and Mongols with an alternation of foreigners present in Tibet until the Chinese managed to install two representatives (amban) in Lhasa. In order to reinstate order throughout the country, with the

30 At the height of their splendour, the Qing emperors of China, who lived in the Forbidden City in Peking (shown in the picture), also ruled over far-off Tibet where they succeeded in establishing a small garrison.

30-31 A determined group from the north of China, the Manchu, began to accumulate power in the middle of the 17th century and, backed with the power of their horseback troops, succeeded in overthrowing the Ming dynasty. On 24 April 1644, the Manchu entered Peking in triumph where they imposed the Qing dynasty.

31 Qianlong, emperor from 1736 to 1795, is considered to have been one of China's greatest rulers. He promoted the arts and culture but was also an excellent strategist and politician. Expanding the borders of the country, he created the largest empire in the world and kept it under his personal control by making regular visits to his territories.

MARE CASPIUM
PERSIA PARS.
ARABIÆ PARS
Sinus Persicus
Ormus
Candahar
Corassan Regn.
Turchestan
Samarcano
Bucara
Cataium
Cotam
Camul
Desertum Lop
Kircassi
REG: CABUL.
REGN. CASCAR.
TIBET REG.
REG: TIBET.
REG: MARANGA.
CASMIR REG.
Guzarale minor.
Caparangue
Agra
Delli
Benares
Bengala
INDIA EXTRA GANGEM.
Tropicus
BENGALA REGN.
Camboia.
Aracam
Pegu Regn.
LAO REGN.
SIAM.
Siam
Guzarate
Sindi
NARSINGA.
Masulipatan
Goa
Cananor
Cochin
Coulan
Candi
ZEILAN
Colombo
Batecalo
Punta de Galle
Maldiva Ins.
OCEANUS
SINUS CAMBOIÆ
Sive
GANGETICUS
INDICUS.
Iter in Chinam
MALACCA
Achem
SUMATRA
CATAIUM tantis apud Geographos motis controversiis, ut vix fuerit qui cum altero de eius situ consentiret: donec complures itinere in illud data opera suscepto, tandem in ipsa CHINA Cataium reperiunt. Quod ut pateat, itinerum a diversis ea de causa susceptorum tractus in hac mappa Geodoporica (in qua tum longitudinum tum latitudinum circuli ad exactiorem itinerum exhibitionem paralleli sunt) disponendos existimavi.

32-33 At the start of the 18th century, missionaries arrived in China and Tibet. These were men of culture as well as faith and they began the mapping of Tibet. Anastasio Kircher was the author of works like Chinae illustratae *and* China Monumentis *written in Latin and illustrated with excellent drawings and maps. Here we see his interpretation of "Cataium" in which he shows the main roads of the time travelled by merchants and missionaries.*

amban they established a small military garrison, and though it hardly seemed important at the time, in fact it signalled the start of Manchu domination that was to last a couple of centuries.

In the meantime, Tibet was becoming more widely known in the west. Its name came from the T.B.T. with which it was referred to in Islamic geography and the country began to appear on maps with ever greater precision. Then, at the start of the 18th century, Jesuit and Capuchin missionaries arrived in Lhasa where they were at first welcomed; they built a mission and even tried to cultivate vines in the lower areas for ritual purposes. The best known of this team of ardent pioneers was the Jesuit Father Ippolito Desiderio from Pistoia in Tuscany. Unlike his brothers, he was

33 top *Another work by Anastasio Kircher shows his missionary colleagues from the Society of Jesus — to which Father Ippolito Desideri also belonged — presenting a map of China at the height of the Jesuits' success and power.*

33 bottom *In Kircher's documents also appears the Potala as a fort built on the mountain and protected at its base by an enclosure wall. Kircher's caption described the palace as "the BIETALA fort where the Great Lama lives".*

In the second half of the century, George Bogle was sent to Tibet by the British, who now occupied India. It was his task to assess the possibility of trading with the country. He was the first Briton to visit Tibet and one of his achievements was the introduction of the potato into Tibetan farming, which directly helped overcome problems of famine.

At the end of the 18th century, the Gurkhas arrived with their army. They succeeded in penetrating deep into the country but the Tibetans requested aid from the Chinese and together the two forces pushed the Gurkhas back. The Qing emperor took advantage of this opportunity to reinforce his military presence and political patronage in Tibet.

a man of great culture and he was respected for his knowledge of the Tibetan language that meant he was able to discuss philosophy and doctrine with the masters of Buddhism. Besides a number of writings in Tibetan, he drew up a weighty document which gave a precise and analytical description of the country. Then, unfortunately, a rivalry arose between the Capuchin and Jesuit orders. The Capuchins, who had won few adepts among their servants, prompted by orders from Rome and fired with zeal, began to attempt conversion of the local population without having much understanding of the Buddhist religion. At first they were denied the friendship of the noble families, then the missionaries were considered universally dangerous and chased out completely.

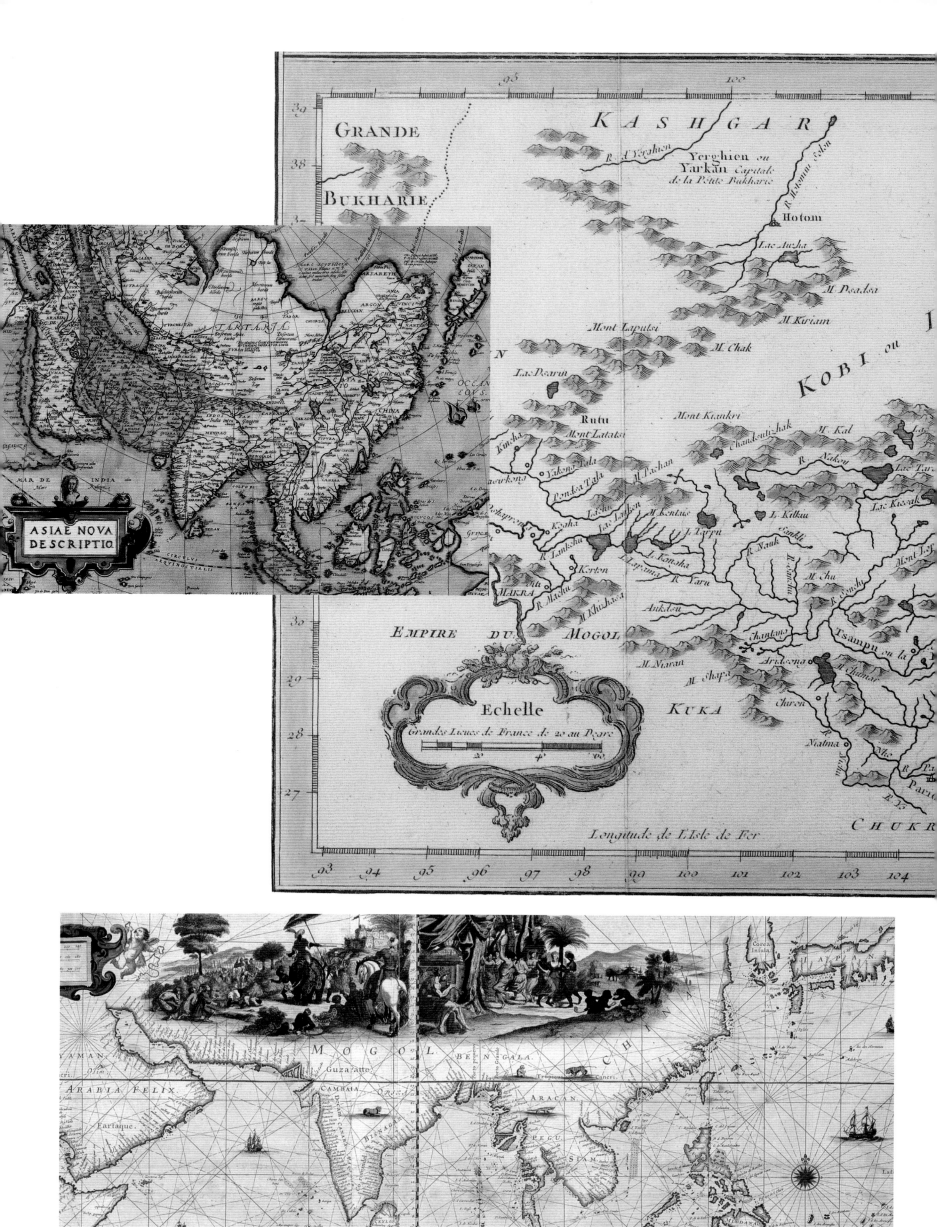

GRANDE
BUKHARIE

KASHGAR

R d'Yerghien
Yerghien ou
Yarkan Capitale
de la Petite Bukharie

Hotom
Lac Aurha

M. Dsadsa
M. Kiriam
Mont Laputsi
M. Chak
KOBI ou
Lac Dearin

Rutu
Mont Krankri
M. Kal
Mont Latatsi
Chandenli hak
R. Nakon
Yakong Tala
M. Pachan
Lac Tan
Ponda Tala
Lac Kiecak
Lichu
M. Kentaie
L. Kilkiu
Koha
Lac Laoken
L. Terpn
R. Nauk
R. Tamksha
I. Kansha
MAKRA
R. Lapina
R. Yaru
M. Chu
Korton
R. Machu
R. Conchu
M. Khuhasa
Ankatsu
Mont Le

EMPIRE DU MOGOL
Chantana
Tsampu ou la
M. Niaran
M. Chapa
Arideong
M. Chonar

Echelle
Grandes Lieues de France de 20 au Degre
KUKA
Chiron

Nialma

Longitude de l'Isle de Fer
CHUKR

ASIAE NOVA
DESCRIPTIO

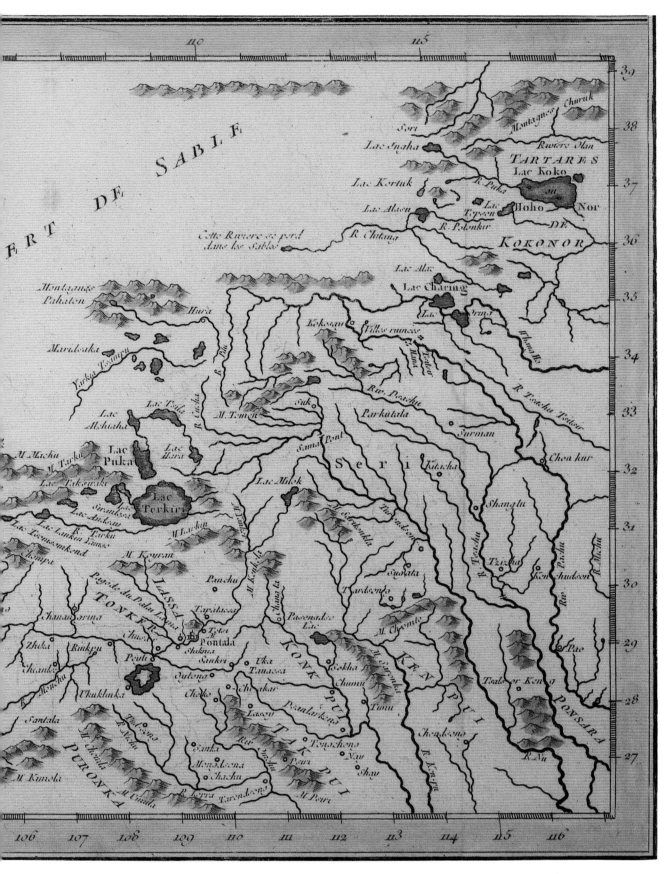

34-35 *As time passed, so map-makers were able to provide more details of inland regions. In this 1749 map with French text, the rivers, chains of mountains and lakes are recognisable. In the centre, the large white area is referred to as the wide "Kobi Desert de Sable".*

34 bottom and 35 bottom *The concept of "Terra Incognita" is evident in the maps of* De Geschiedenis van de Kartografie *printed in Amsterdam respectively in 1670 and 1700. Here the problem of the unknown lands north of the Himalayas was resolved by painting picturesque scenes of costumes and armies on the move.*

34 top *Western map-making took great leaps forward following the trips made by European explorers. One of the principal cartographers was Abraham Ortelius who wanted to present as faithful a picture as possible of the known world in 148 engraved plates in his 1595* Theatrum Orbis Terrarum. *In* Asiae Nova Descriptione, *Tibet is not yet indicated.*

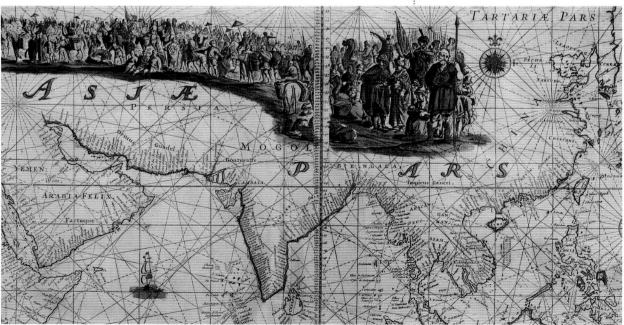

Tibet between myth and history 35

36 Tibetan thangka *and frescoes representing spiritual or political centres decorate the walls of large temples. This fresco in Potala palace depicts the Jokhang.*

36-37 top *The arrangement of the buildings in the oldest images less illustrates their geographical siting than a religious interpretation. This is the Potala, high up on the red hill and in a central position, surrounded by the three monastic centres – Drepung, Sera and Ganden – in a crowded setting of trees, animals and people.*

36-37 bottom *This ancient map of Lhasa seems more faithful to the geography of the city. It shows the Potala palace with its walls and gates and the square layout of the Jokhang temple with its golden roofs. The uncultivated land between them is marked by roads and paths and dotted with small houses and temples in a manner that was typical of Lhasa for centuries.*

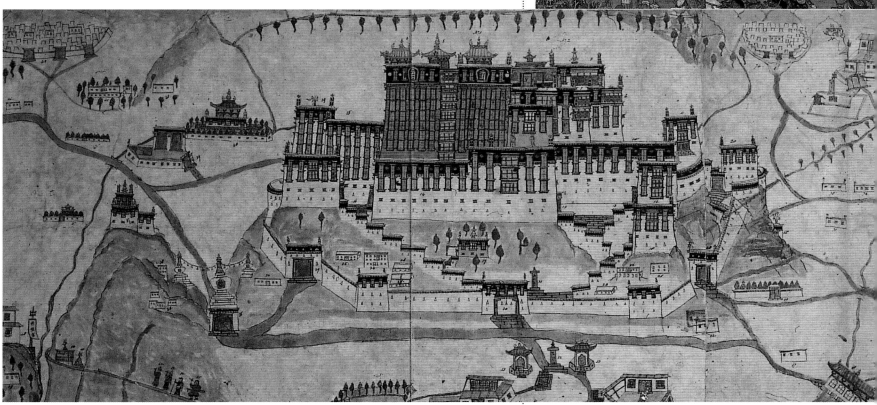

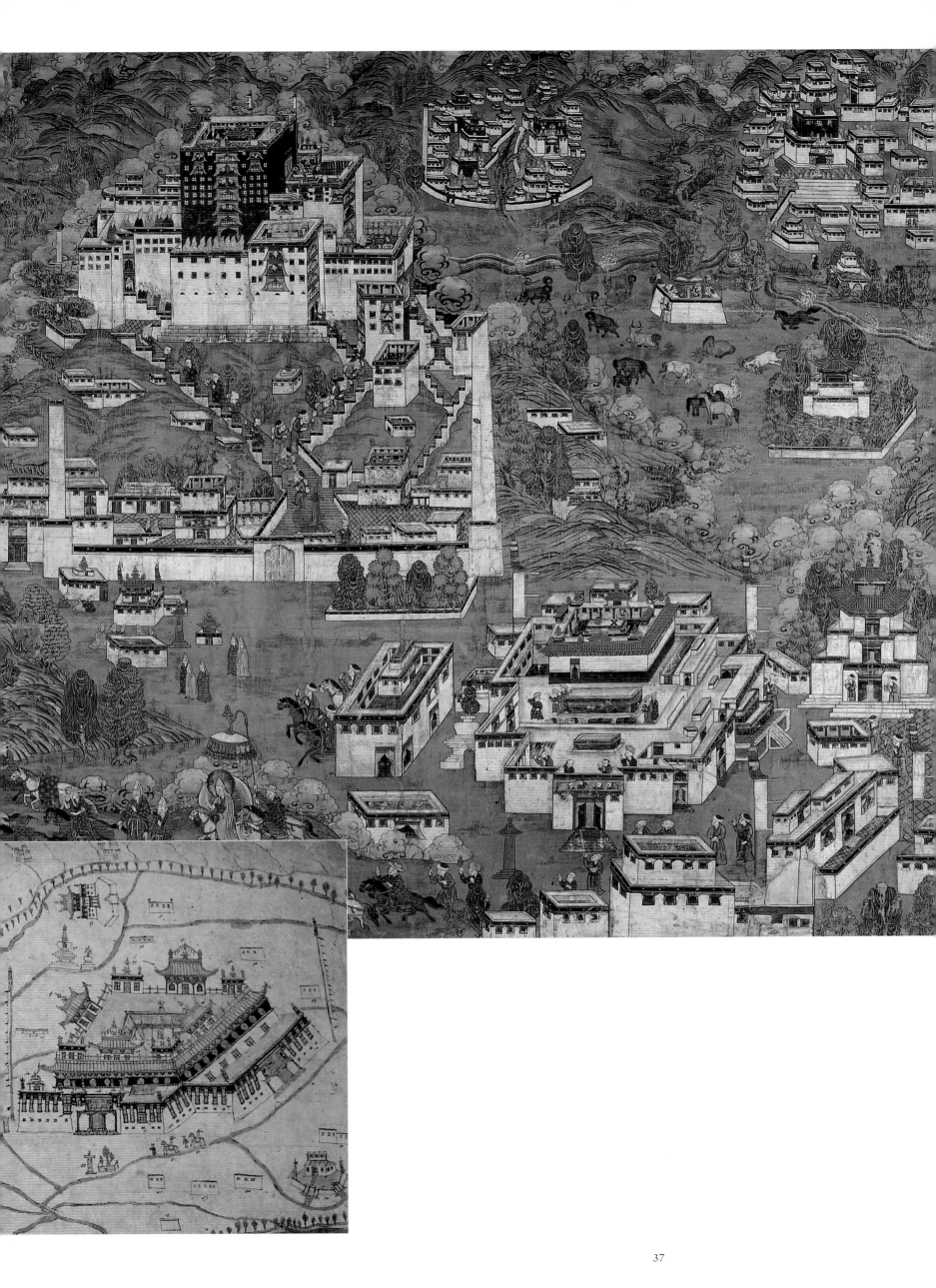

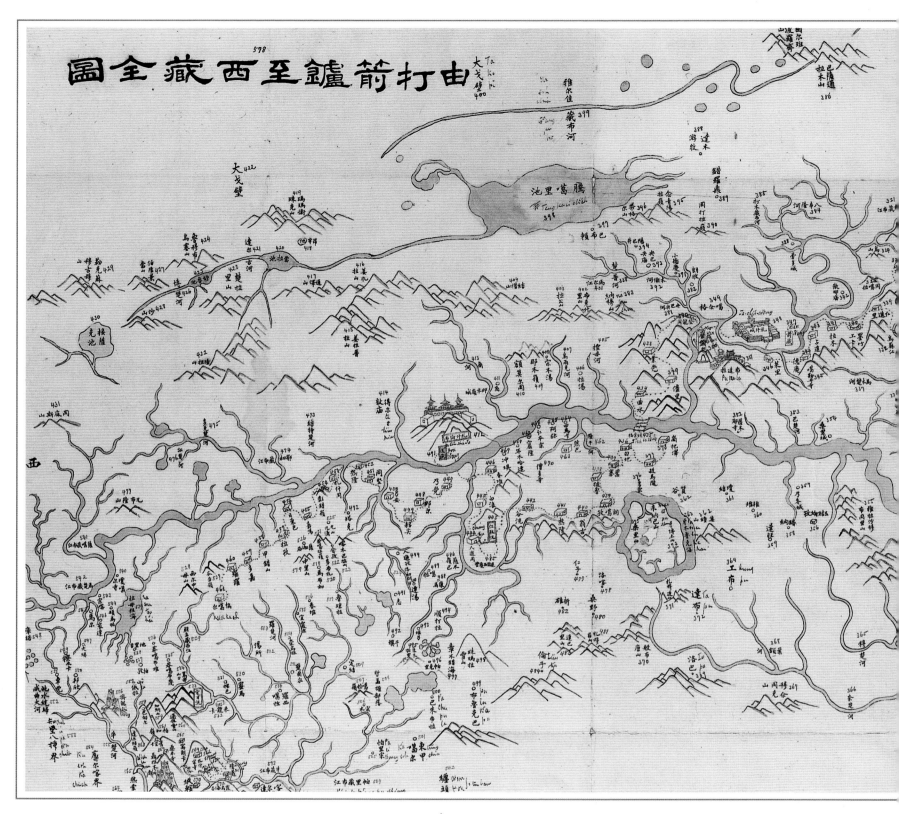

圖全藏西至鑪箭打由

38-39 *The Chinese also had a long and good tradition of map-making. This ancient but undated map shows the course of the Brahmaputra river and Lake Yamdrok tsho with its rounded branches. The captions are written in ancient Chinese.*

39 bottom *Following explorations and geographic discoveries in central regions of Asia, the Royal Geographical Society published an 1875 map of Tibet and Nepal in Volume 15 which showed the routes of native explorers.*
The land north of the Brahmaputra was given the generic name of "Great Tibet".

圖全藏西至鑪箭打由

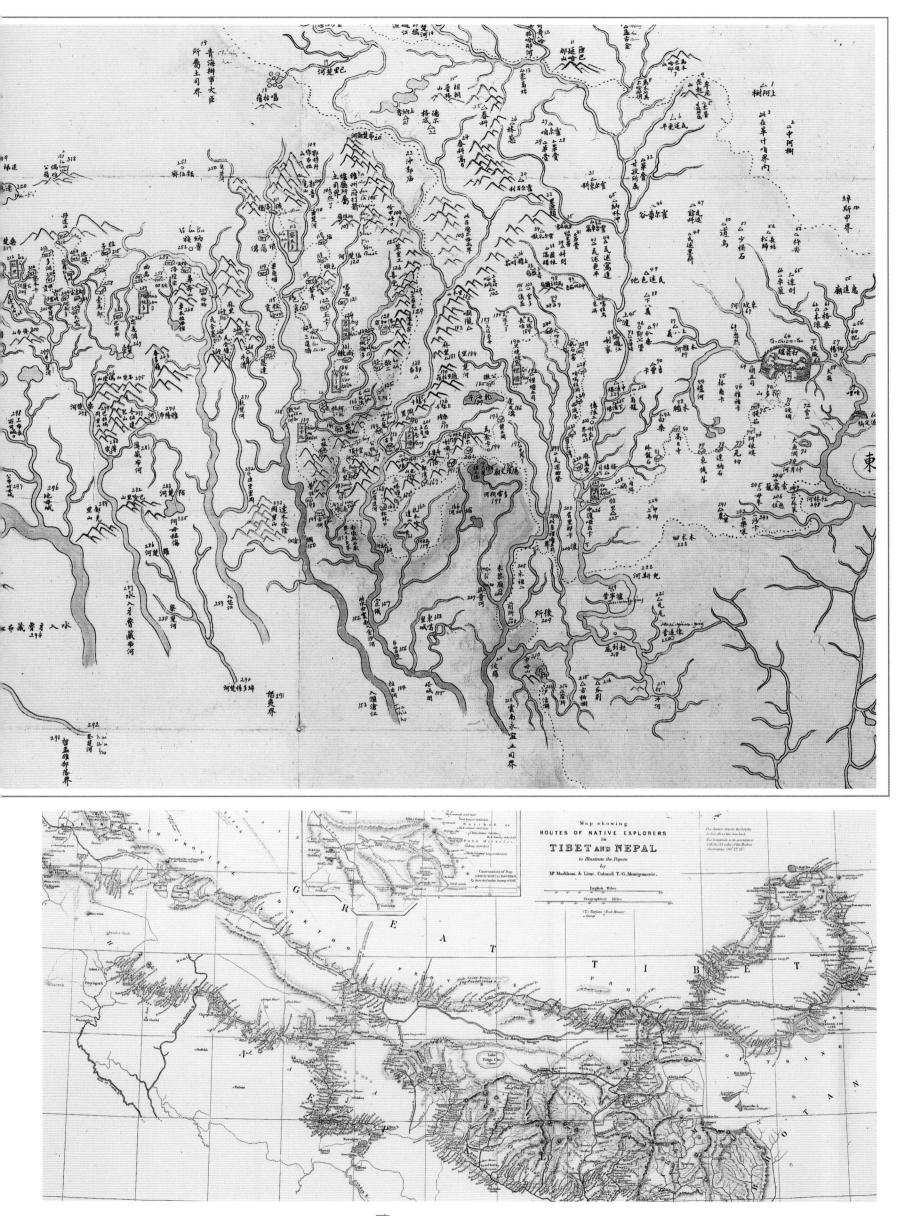

40-41 *Despite being part of the Chinese Empire, Tibet, Mongolia and Manchuria were considered as external territories in this map published by J. & F. Tallis in 1851 and therefore separated by border lines. Among the various images that characterise the different countries, the Potala palace can be seen at the bottom right.*

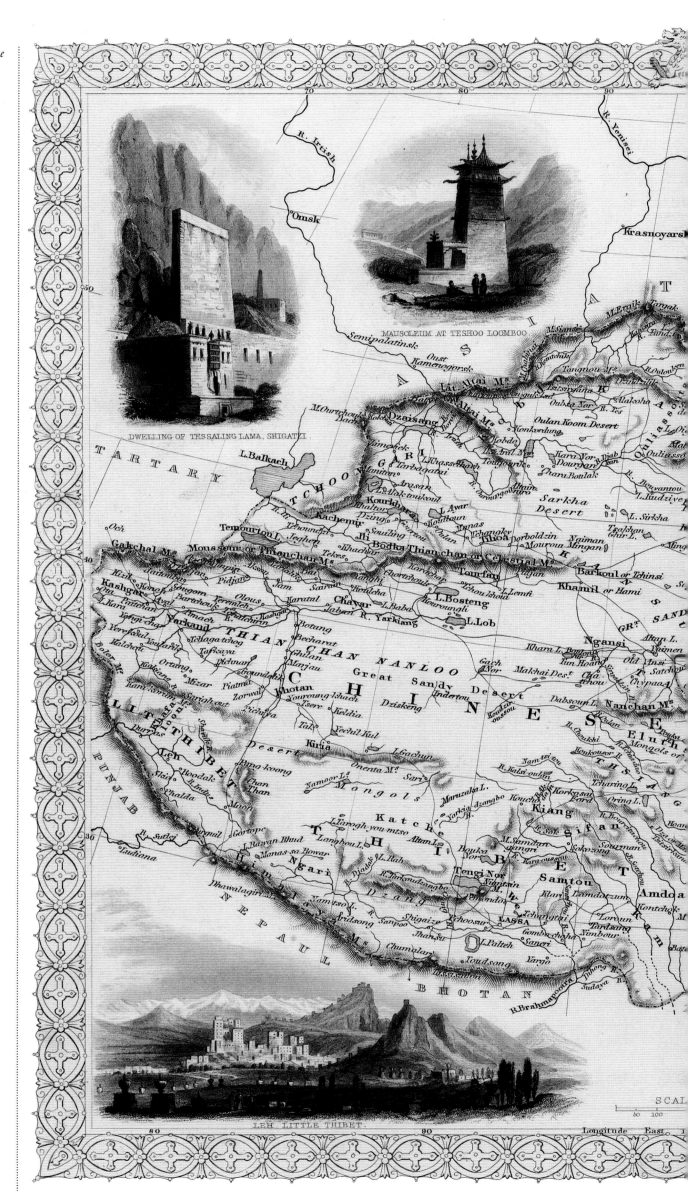

DWELLING OF TESSALING LAMA, SHIGATZI.

MAUSOLEUM AT TESHOO LOOMBOO

LEH LITTLE THIBET.

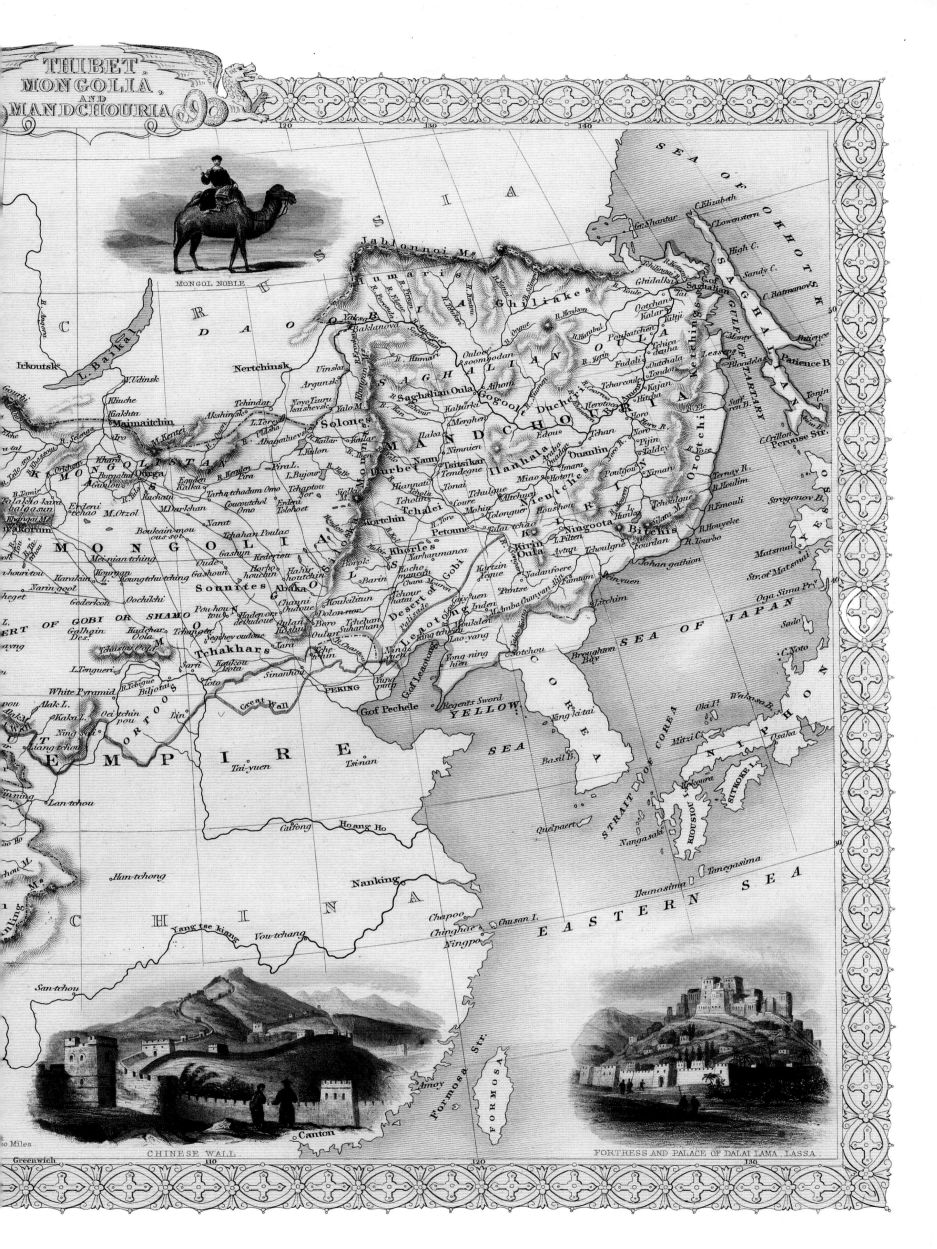

THIBET, MONGOLIA, AND MANDCHOURIA

MONGOL NOBLE

SEA OF OKHOTSK

R U S S I A

C. Elizabeth
Lowenstern
High C.
Sandy C.
C. Ratmanov's.

Jablonnoi Ms.

Kumaris
Ghilirakes
Gr. Shantar

GULF OF TARTARY
SAGHALIAN

Patience B.

Irkoutsk
L. Baikal
DAOURIA
Gof Saghalian
Perouse Str.

Nertchinsk
V. Udinsk
Kliuche
Argunsk
Tchindat
Akshinsk
SAGHALIAN OULA
GOGOOL
DUCHERI
MANDCHOURIA

C. Crillon
C. Romanov's.

Maimaitchin
Solones
Perouse Str.

MONGOLISTAN
Ourga
Durbet
ILANHALA
Nieutche
KIRIN
OROTCHI KETCHIS

MONGOLIA
Sounites
Abaka
Khorles
Petoune
Kirin Oula
Ningoota
Birthis

DESERT OF GOBI OR SHAMO
Desert of Gobi
Leaotong
SEA OF JAPAN

Thakhars
Sinanhou
Great Wall
PEKING

EMPIRE
Gof Pechele
Regents Sword
YELLOW
COREA
NIPHON

Tai-yuen
Tsinan
SEA
Basil B.
STRAIT OF COREA

C H I N A
Hoang Ho
Cuifong
Nanking
Quelpaert
Nangasaki

Han-tchong
Lan-tchou
Yang tse kiang
Vou-tchang
Ningpo
Chapoo
Chinghde
Chusan I.

EASTERN SEA

San-tchou
Amoy
FORMOSA

Canton

CHINESE WALL

FORTRESS AND PALACE OF DALAI LAMA, LASSA.

The various 19th-century Dalai Lamas all died young so political and administrative power remained in the hands of regents. Consequently, Tibet experienced a period of stagnation and internal disputes while China, also weakened by internal conflict and the advance of the western world's colonial aims, gradually reduced its influence in Tibet.

In 1876, the 13th Dalai Lama was born, a figure who was to leave his mark on a Tibet that was beginning to appear of great interest to the eyes of western powers expanding in Asia. Britain and Russia in particular sent agents, more or less incognito, to win the favour of the God-Ruler. In 1903, the situation became so complex and tense that Britain decided to send a military expedition with the aim of opening a diplomatic office in Lhasa. The expedition, organised by the Viceroy of India, Lord Curzon, was led by Colonel Francis Younghusband. It entered Tibet from Sikkim and

42 top Records of Tibet became more accurate with the invention of the camera. In September 1910, this photograph of the 13th Dalai Lama was published in the London newspaper, The Sphere. It was the first picture of the God-Ruler to appear in the western world.

42 bottom The government of the Dalai Lama was made up of monks and distinguished lay people. If the God-Ruler was not of age or was absent, his council appointed a regent to take his place. The photograph shows four members of the 13th Dalai Lama's government.

43 top left The small Chinese garrison installed in Lhasa in 1717 by the Qing dynasty was directed by two amban. They remained in Tibet until the fall of the Qing dynasty in the execution of their formal duty as liaisons and advisors.

43 top right Francis Younghusband was the commander of the famous 1904 expedition sent to Tibet by the Indian Viceroy to open a diplomatic office in Lhasa. Great Britain's purpose in doing so was also to slow the Russian initiatives about which rumours had filtered through.

43 centre right Before taking any decisions, the Dalai Lama's government used to consult the state oracle in Nechung monastery. During a complex and secret ceremony, the oracle-monk would fall into a trance and voice the prediction.

43 bottom right British troops reached Lhasa in August 1904 and entered the city passing below the great chorten. Colonel Younghusband was unable to meet the Dalai Lama, who had fled to Mongolia.

43 bottom left The British on their way to Lhasa had originally entered Tibet via Sikkim but, finding that no representation was made to them by the Tibetan government, they headed for Gyantse. There they were met by a poorly armed and organised defence and entered the fort on 6 July 1904.

stayed for a while in the Chumbi Valley just beyond the border but, as no-one approached the British from the Tibetan government, the troops headed for Gyantse where they launched a few mortar shells, routed the poorly armed and organised defence and entered the fort. From there they moved on to Lhasa where they found that the Dalai Lama had fled to Mongolia with his Russian advisors. Negotiations directed by the Regent followed which led to an agreement whereby the British withdrew. The treaty recognised Tibet's right to sovereign rule but was only signed by the Tibetans and the British, not by the Manchu.

In 1911, the revolution that led to the downfall of the Qing dynasty broke out in China and this gave the Dalai Lama the chance to chase out the *amban* and make his country independent. This state of affairs was to last some decades even if China never recognised Tibet's independence formally.

However, the country remained closed to the outside world in a "splendid" and highly idealised political and cultural isolation which was to bring heavy consequences.

Although the country was closed to foreigners, there were individuals who succeeded in entering Tibet for different motives. For the most part they were the explorers who were to become famous for their descriptions and early photographic documentation of the country. This handful of people gave the western world an idea of the

44-45 top Sven Hedin, the great Swedish traveller of the early 20th century, not only left valuable written documentation of his discoveries but also excellent drawings, sketches and watercolours. This is Lake Porutsho, situated at nearly 17,000 feet north of the Transhimalaya chain that Hedin made known to the western world with his brush.

44 centre and bottom left As he advanced into the heart of the unknown land, Sven Hedin was stopped and prevented from proceeding by Tibetan soldiers. The soldiers, noted Hedin, "ran wildly in front, behind and between the tents as though they wanted to throw us to the ground".

45 top and centre Even the monasteries in remote areas entered western imagination thanks to the art of the Swedish traveller. Here we see the monastery of Mendong with a group of monks and the monastery of Nganglaring covered with prayer flags.

45 bottom right Sven Hedin often travelled wearing local clothes as they offered two benefits: centuries of trial and error had produced a cut that gave best protection from the elements and, more important, he was less conspicuous. Yet, despite his precautions, he was stopped on his journey.

44 centre and bottom right, 45 bottom left Once more using his watercolours, Hedin reproduced the clothes and ornaments of Tibetan women in the Transhimalaya. This world of exotic costumes and habits enchanted the western public and fostered the myth of Tibet.

unknown and mythical country and allowed the modern world to understand Tibet and its people of the time. One of the most famous was Sven Hedin, the Swedish traveller who succeeded in penetrating the steppes of central Asia at the start of the 20th century and in reaching deep into Tibet. Although he did not reached all the destinations he had in mind, he arrived in Chang Thang, crossed the large mountain chain north of the Brahmaputra (which he named Transhimalaya) and stopped for some time in Shigatse where he became friend of the Panchen Lama. He did not, however, receive permission to go to Lhasa. A careful observer and excellent painter as well as writer, he left a remarkable collection of drawings and watercolours that for a long time in the west were considered the only documentation of the distant and unknown land.

Tibet between myth and history

46 While awaiting permission to travel on to Lhasa, Sven Hedin stayed at length in Shigatse which he documented with great talent. His watercolours show the entrance to the mausoleum that contains the tomb of the fifth Panchen Lama (top), a high lama (bottom left) and the image of Tsongkhapa on the altar at Namgyal Lhakang (bottom right).

47 bottom left The mausoleum of the first Panchen Lama faces onto the large courtyard that, even at the time of Sven Hedin, was the setting for holy representations in front of large numbers of spectators.

47 top left, 47 bottom right, 47 bottom left Among the many portraits by Sven Hedin are those of the abbot of Selipuk, the monks of Mendong and the Panchen Lama, who became the traveller's friend.

Ekai Kawaguchi, the Japanese Buddhist, was a famous pilgrim who went to Tibet to study the holy doctrine and translate it into Japanese. He remained in Tibet for three years and was in Lhasa at the time that the intrigues between the British and Russian agents flared up which led to the Younghusband expedition. Kawaguchi remained involved in the situation to the point that he himself was suspected of being a spy until, obeying a mysterious voice – he later recounted – he understood it was time to leave the country.

A few years later, Alexandra David Néel also arrived in Tibet where she remained uninterruptedly from 1914-1924 and was the first western woman to enter the Forbidden City. A writer, journalist and former singer, helped by a loving and understanding husband, she disguised herself as a common Tibetan woman and shared life with local people of all types. She learnt the mysteries of their esoteric and attractive religion and left exceptional photographs and descriptions

48-49 In one of the first photographs, taken in 1887, the valley of Lhasa seems little populated around the Potala which rises massively on Marpori hill. The Tibetan village of Shöl is spread out at its feet and two monks play tungchen *in the foreground.*

48 centre The monks in charge of security display their tools to the camera of Heinrich Harrer: a long wooden stick for the servants and a sharpened metal rod with central grip for the "guards" which they used to control the crowds during religious ceremonies.

48 bottom As required by the Dalai Lama's government, there were also two governors at Gyantse. Although both were of equal rank, the monk occupies a slightly higher seat. This picture comes from the extensive collection of photographs taken by Heinrich Harrer.

49 top Alexandra David Néel was an extraordinary traveller who disguised herself as a Tibetan in order to move around the country unrecognised. By wearing a chupa, colouring her face, often with soot, and benefiting from an excellent mastery of the Tibetan language, she was able to become the "Parisienne in Lhasa" when the city was closed to all westerners.

49 bottom With the full page publication of this picture of monks with long trumpets on 29 February 1908, the London newspaper The Sphere gave the news that the British expedition led by Colonel Francis Younghusband was leaving Tibet after a three-year stay in the border area.

50 top left Today known to the public via the media, Heinrich Harrer reached Tibet during World War II where he remained for seven years. An expert mountain climber and great sportsman, he is seen here as he skates on a frozen section of the river Kyichu below Chakpori hill. His many photographs provide superb documentation of Tibetan society as it was before the arrival of the Chinese.

of the country.

At the start of the 1920's, English mountain climbing expeditions also arrived with the aim of finding a way up Everest. They were accompanied by Colonel Howard Bury, a naturalist and writer, who produced accurate documentation especially of the Himalayan territories. The most learned of Italian specialists of Tibet, Giuseppe Tucci, arrived at the start of the 1930's. This indefatigable traveller and rigorous scientist made many trips up to the 1950's and left an immense amount of written and photographic documentation occasionally with the help of the photographer, Colonel Eugenio Ghersi, and the naturalist, writer and photographer, Fosco Maraini.

Heinrich Harrer, whose exploits have been made known chiefly through the media, was an Austrian mountain-climber who escaped from a concentration camp in India during World War II and reached Tibet where he stayed for seven years. He was welcomed by the Tibetan authorities and was admitted to high society where he witnessed various events that left their mark on life in the capital at that time. Equipped with a good quality camera, he put together documentation that became a milestone in the history of knowledge of Tibet in its last years as a theocratic state.

The 14th and current Dalai Lama was born in 1935. Internal diatribes and the increasingly incumbent presence of China forced him to take the

50 top right *Tibetan boats made with yak skin were widely used to transport goods and people along the local rivers. This picture shows some members of the government on an inspection trip.*

50 bottom *These two ladies in ceremonial dress are, on the left, a minister's wife who is wearing the costume and hat of the Tsang district, and, on the right, her daughter-in-law who is wearing the dress and head-covering typical of the Ü, the region in which Lhasa lies.*

51 top *Tibetans have always loved playing games. Grouped around a table with dice and white shells used for keeping score, apart from the photographer Heinrich Harrer, there are Tibetan ministerial advisers and two diplomats, one English and one Sikkimese.*

51 centre *The large silk* thangka *embroidered with the figure of Buddha was hung on a wall of the Potala during important festivals when prayers, music and sacred dances were celebrated by all the inhabitants of the city.*

51 bottom *The procedure related to the principle of reincarnation requires that once the deceased has been recognised in a child, the child has to leave the house of his parents to be educated by monks. The photograph shows the reincarnation of the founder of the Drigung sect, recognised at the age of three, as he is being taken to his monastery.*

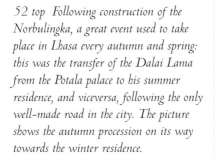

52 top Following construction of the Norbulingka, a great event used to take place in Lhasa every autumn and spring: this was the transfer of the Dalai Lama from the Potala palace to his summer residence, and viceversa, following the only well-made road in the city. The picture shows the autumn procession on its way towards the winter residence.

52 centre The God-Ruler was carried on a litter carried by twelve men with a shade of peacock feathers carried in front and a brocade shade behind. As the Dalai Lama was still a minor when Heinrich Harrer was present in Tibet, the shade of the regent was also carried in the procession to display his own importance.

52 bottom Ministers and dignitaries followed on horseback. This group of riders are wearing clothes and head-coverings that distinguish them as laymen from the government.

53 bottom During the procession, the most important prelates also rode on horseback wearing splendid brocade vestments and hats that distinguished them as high lamas.

53 left The Dalai Lama's horse, decked out in festival decorations, was also part of the procession but did not carry its regal rider. Instead it was preceded by a top ranking abbot.

53 top right The crowd waited impatiently for the procession on either side of the street. When the Dalai Lama himself passed, everyone bowed down to the ground to avert their eyes from the "fount of blessings".

THE CHILD RULER COMES TO LHASA :
HOMAGE TO THE NEW FOUR-YEAR-OLD DALAI LAMA.

THE DALAI LAMA, THE NEW INCARNATION OF AVALOKITESVARA, THE ANCESTOR OF THE TIBETANS, NEARS HIS CAPITAL : THE PROCESSION AND THE PALANQUIN IN WHICH THE CHILD TRAVELLED.

THE YELLOW AND BLUE PEACOCK TENT IN WHICH THE REINCARNATED DALAI LAMA RECEIVED THE HOMAGE OF THE REGENT AND OTHER OFFICIALS—INCLUDING BRITISH REPRESENTATIVES.

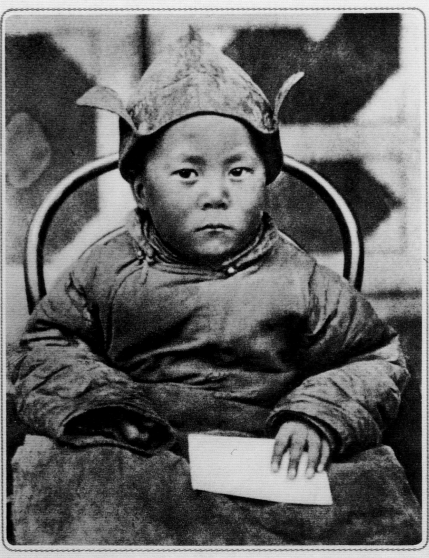

THE NEW DALAI LAMA : THE FOUR-YEAR-OLD PEASANT CHILD FROM THE DISTANT PROVINCE OF SILLING, THE FOURTEENTH INCARNATION OF THE BODDHISATVA AVALOKITESVARA.

THE ENCAMPMENT ON A PLAIN BELOW ROCKY FOOTHILLS WHICH WAS THE SCENE OF THE FIRST CEREMONY ON THE ARRIVAL OF THE DALAI LAMA ; THE PEACOCK TENT BEING IN THE CENTRE SURROUNDED WITH OTHER TENTS LAID OUT IN SQUARES.

The new Dalai Lama of Tibet arrived at Lhasa early in October. The new ruler is, of course, a child. He is four years old and was found in the distant Chinese province of Silling. Tibetans believe him to be the reincarnation of their compassionate ruler Chenrezi. On his way to Lhasa (whither he was accompanied by his father and mother and two brothers) the child rested at the monastery of Rigya, some two miles away. The Regent of Tibet went in procession to Rigya to await his coming. After a short rest at Rigya the child was carried down to receive homage in the Peacock Tent. When he was seated on the throne the officials, headed by the Regent, began to file past him offering white scarves and receiving his blessing. Those appearing before him included British, Nepalese, and Chinese representatives. " The dignity and self-possession of the child impressed everyone " writes a special correspondent of " The Times " who was present : " He looked about calmly, seeming unmoved by the magnificence, and as if he were in familiar surroundings. Although appearing to grow tired towards the end of the ceremony he did not lose his composure. He never smiled, but maintained a placid, equable gaze. Much of his attention was directed to a calm inspection of members of the British Mission, as though he were trying to recall where he had seen such people before."

PHOTOGRAPHS BY THE CHINA INLAND MISSION ; AND " THE TIMES."

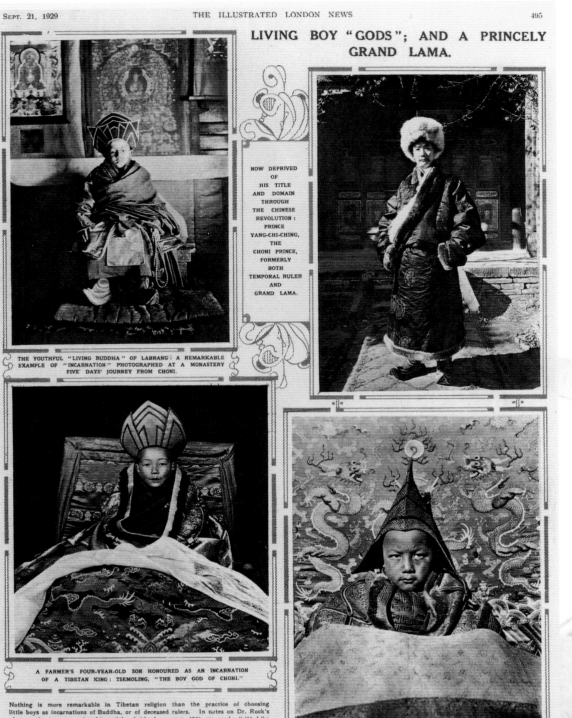

LIVING BOY "GODS"; AND A PRINCELY GRAND LAMA.

THE YOUTHFUL "LIVING BUDDHA" OF LABRANG: A REMARKABLE EXAMPLE OF "INCARNATION" PHOTOGRAPHED AT A MONASTERY FIVE DAYS' JOURNEY FROM CHONI.

NOW DEPRIVED OF HIS TITLE AND DOMAIN THROUGH THE CHINESE REVOLUTION: PRINCE YANG-CHI-CHING, THE CHONI PRINCE, FORMERLY BOTH TEMPORAL RULER AND GRAND LAMA.

A FARMER'S FOUR-YEAR-OLD SON HONOURED AS AN INCARNATION OF A TIBETAN KING: TSEMOLING, "THE BOY GOD OF CHONI."

A LITTLE BOY OF SIX WHO RULES OVER A MONASTERY A FEW MILES SOUTH-WEST OF CHONI: THE "LIVING BUDDHA" OF GUYA.

Nothing is more remarkable in Tibetan religion than the practice of choosing little boys as incarnations of Buddha, or of deceased rulers. In notes on Dr. Rock's photographs (accompanying his article abridged on page 494), we read: "(1) Like Choni and Guya, Labrang has recently installed a boy god. This young Living Buddha was photographed at Angkur, Gomba, a monastery five days' journey to the north of Choni."—2. If a Prince has two sons, the elder succeeds him, and the second becomes grand lama in the monastery; but if there is only one son, he takes both positions concurrently. Prince Yang Chi-ching (the Choni Prince) is both temporal ruler and grand lama. . . . He was exceedingly hospitable. He gave orders to the lamas to aid me in taking photographs, and not only admitted me to all religious ceremonies, but gave me the place of honour." (In a subsequent letter, Dr. Rock stated that, since his departure, the Choni Prince had been shorn of his title and rank, and his domain had been confiscated by Feng Yu-shiang, the Red General. The Prince had become merely a "com-missioner of barbarians.")—(3) The Dalai Lama declared this four-year-old son of a poor farmer the incarnation of the Tibetan King who died shortly before Dr. Rock's arrival.—(4) The "Living Buddha" of Guya is six years old. The monastery over which this solemn little fellow rules is a few miles from Choni."

PHOTOGRAPHS BY DR. JOSEPH F. ROCK. REPRODUCED BY COURTESY OF THE NATIONAL GEOGRAPHIC SOCIETY, OF WASHINGTON, U.S.A. (SEE ARTICLE ON PAGE 494.)

54-55 In 1939, the Illustrated London News *dedicated a whole page to the Dalai Lama and his coronation in Lhasa in the presence of British, Nepalese and Chinese guests. In 1929, a page had been dedicated to the reincarnated Lamas in eastern Tibet that had begun to be involved in events in the Chinese civil war.*

These were two of the earliest presentations of Tibet to the curiosity of the western public. For the west, this represented the discovery of a world of magic that was to increase as the years passed but which, at the same time, marked the approach to its destruction.

56 top "Heavenly funerals" are still celebrated in Tibet. In a country that has little wood and land that is hard and frozen for much of the year, the solution of offering the body of the deceased for the benefit of living beings is logical and in keeping with the principles of Buddhism. This photograph was taken by Chandra Das, the Indian diplomat who was in Tibet between 1879 and 1882 and the author, among other works, of a famous Tibetan-English dictionary.

56 bottom Even if some members of the government recognised the need to modernise the army, the Tibetan government as a whole felt the position of the country was safe and invested little in defence. This choice was to have far-reaching consequences in the years to come.

57 top left *At one time minstrels were common in Tibet when they toured villages and played a single-stringed instrument to accompany the songs and dances of their company. As Tibet had no means of communication, strolling players like these were also the means by which news was spread from one village to the next.*

57 top right *Another of Sven Hedin's sketches shows a monk with a* kangling, *an instrument used in Tantric ceremonies made from a human tibia.*

57 bottom right *Sven Hedin's caption describes this picture as a portrait of "a boy injured by a rifle shot".*

57 bottom left *The Tibetan practice of stretching out the tongue almost as far as the chin as a mode of greeting disconcerted the first western travellers. As the custom became more widely known, the practice became rarer and is now almost unused by the young.*

reins of the country when he was only sixteen. On 1 October 1949 after a long civil war, the victorious Communist leader Mao Zedong declared in Tian'anmen Square that China had risen to its feet. This also signified claims of China's rights over territories that had in some way been under the dominion of the Qing dynasty and, consequently, in 1950 Mao sent an army to claim Tibet as part of China. The Tibetan army was routed and in 1951 representatives of the country's government were sent to Peking where they signed the still controversial "17 Point Agreement". This meant that Tibet formally accepted Chinese sovereignty while Tibet was recognised as having full regional autonomy. In an extremely difficult situation, the Dalai Lama approved this agreement and for some years attempted to find a solution for Tibetans within the form of autonomy that China had conceded. But the situation gradually deteriorated until, in 1959, a revolt broke out in Lhasa which was bloodily put down. The Dalai Lama and one hundred thousand Tibetans fled the country to settle in India where he founded a community and a government in exile that for years has done

58 top In 1951, the situation in Tibet changed completely when the Communist party took power. The photograph shows a Chinese Communist official reading a proclamation to the residents of Lhasa in front of the Potala.

58 centre Before surrendering to the Chinese, Tibetans attempted both negotiation and force. Heinrich Harrer's photograph shows the younger brother of minister Surkhang trying to handle a machine gun.

58 bottom Modestly armed, the Tibetan army attempted to combine their own traditions with whatever they had gleaned from the British military. In this photograph, Tibetan troops are presenting arms.

59 top right The two flags best-loved by Tibetans were taken by the Dalai Lama on his journey into exile: his personal standard and the flag of Tibet with the rising sun and snow lions.

59 bottom In 1951, the PLA (People's Liberation Army) entered Lhasa to "liberate the oppressed Tibetan people and reunite them with the mother country".

59 top left The position of the Dalai Lama became increasingly difficult with the Chinese on Tibetan soil. While trying to oversee co-existence within the scope permitted by the 17 Point Agreement, the Dalai Lama travelled to Peking with the Panchen Lama in 1954 where he met Mao Zedong. It was an historic event but produced no longlasting solution.

60 top This is the last photograph taken by Heinrich Harrer of the Dalai Lama in Tibet. The God-Ruler is receiving the golden urn that contains a reliquary of Buddha.

60 bottom The Dalai Lama left Lhasa for India in December 1959 accompanied by forty nobles and escorted by two hundred armed soldiers. Their long and difficult march took them over the Himalayas and through the forests of Assam.

everything in its power to keep the Tibetan culture strong and to find a political solution to the Tibet problem.

In 1965 the Autonomous Region of Tibet was founded and Communist social reforms were systematically put in place; Chinese *han* – common people and state cadres – began to arrive from China but they did not integrate with the local population. Public works such as the construction of bridges, roads, electric power stations and schools were undertaken and agricultural communes were set up which should have provided work and food for all in equal measure. The Cultural Revolution exploded throughout China from 1967 to 1969 affecting Tibet too; monasteries, books and parts of the country's cultural heritage were destroyed and a huge number of people died. Food shortages, disorder, factional struggles and terror

dominated the country until 1976 when the political scene changed with Mao's death. Deng Xiao-ping, who followed a more pragmatic line, was confirmed as leader in 1978. He left the Cultural Revolution behind him and set about bringing changes to Tibet. In 1980 the Chinese Prime Minister, Hu Yaobang, made an official visit to the country during which he admitted the failure of the communes and the disasters caused by the Cultural Revolution and launched a programme of reforms; one of these was that central government intended to deal with the various requests in consultation with the local people and that "the adoption of a private system matched to Tibetan circumstances" was to be undertaken. The communes were dissolved, land and animal stocks were divided among families, social, education and health programmes were put in place and were even created institutions to restore Tibet's cultural heritage.

This period of relative openness lasted until the end of the 1980's when revolts and repression in Tibet, coupled with the tragedy in Tian'enman Square in Peking, signalled the start of a new phase which was to characterise the 1990's. While the *han* population continued to increase both in number

61 top On 16 May 1959 after six days of fighting, the citizens of Lhasa surrendered. The long column of insurgents left the city en route for the Chinese camp preceded by symbols of their surrender. This picture was only recently sent to London by Chinese Communist sources.

61 centre The Dalai Lama and his fleeing company had to cross Himalayan passes on their journey to India. Here we see the Dalai Lama, the sixth from the left, during a rest stop.

61 bottom The Dalai Lama left Tibet secretly, dressed as a simple soldier. After an adventuruous crossing of south-eastern Tibet and the Himalayas, he succeeded in finding refuge in India. There he established his official seat in the district of Dharamsala where he and thousands of exiled Tibetans still live.

Tibet between myth and history 61

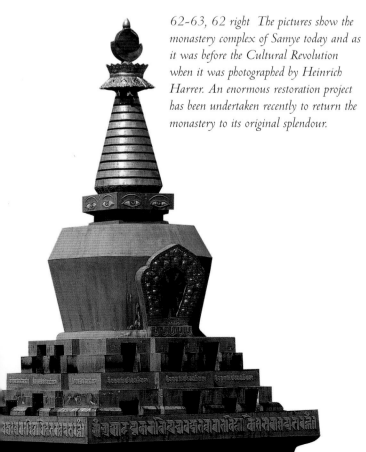

62-63, 62 right The pictures show the monastery complex of Samye today and as it was before the Cultural Revolution when it was photographed by Heinrich Harrer. An enormous restoration project has been undertaken recently to return the monastery to its original splendour.

63 centre right The Cultural Revolution did not only unleash its anger on Ganden but also on the other monastic cities. Almost all the monks disappeared, many of which were forced into secular life, and the walls were torn down. This is a view of the ruins of Drepung.

63 bottom left and 63 bottom right In order to erase the past, the Cultural Revolution destroyed all the religious symbols it could find: statues, books and frescoes produced during centuries of cultural and spiritual life disappeared forever.

62 left The restoration also includes reconstruction of the four large chorten but in cement rather than the traditional stone, wood and other local materials for reasons of economy. A final coat of paint produces a result that, seen from a distance, is actually rather attractive.

63 top left, 63 centre left, 63 top right Ganden was one of the places that suffered most during the tragedies of the 1960's. Here it is seen at its maximum splendour in the 1949 photograph by Hugh Richardson (top), after it was sacked during the Cultural Revolution (left) and partially rebuilt (right).

64 top, 64-65 The photographs show the results of the Cultural Revolution at the fort of Lhatse. Only a few ruins of the ancient fort remain from which the local inhabitants still regularly hang festoons of prayer flags.

65 top and 65 centre top Shigatse fort, seat of the lords of Tsang, was the site of the famous meeting in 1642 between the fifth Dalai Lama and the defeated lord of Tsang after which the dominance of the theocratic state of the Dalai Lama began. Today, as can be seen in the picture, the fort is in ruins and a modern city of glass and cement lies at its feet beyond Tashilhunpo.

65 centre right and 65 bottom right Gyantse fort was the centre of an important trading city on the road from Sikkim to Lhasa. Today, the fort is in ruins, the border with Sikkim is closed to foreigners and Lhasa and Shigatse are linked by a road that follows the Brahmaputra gorges so all that is left to the ancient and noble Gyantse is the beauty of its buildings.

66 top Modern Lhasa has about 200,000 inhabitants and its monuments are almost hidden by the huddle of surrounding buildings.

66-67 In 1988, a year before his death, the Panchen Lama returned to Lhasa and climbed on the roof of the Jokhang to bless the crowd in the square below.

66 centre Mr. Raidi is Vice Executive Secretary of the party of the Autonomous Region of Tibet and one of the most powerful administrators in the country.

66 bottom During the 1980's, Deng Xiao-ping, centre, and Hu Yaobang, right, carried forward a pragmatic policy that reconfirmed the rights of ethnic minorities within the large, multi-ethnic Chinese state.

and as an economic force, unity with the mother country was emphatically stated in every corner of the land in the face of every real or presumed movement in the direction of separatism. A milestone of this political line was the Third Forum on Work in Tibet which was held in Peking from 20-23 July 1994. Comments, published in Lhasa's daily newspaper *Xizang Ribao* on 6 September 1994, by Raidi, the executive vice-secretary of the party of the Autonomous Region of Tibet, were as follows: "Tibet's reform must conform with the framework for ongoing reform of the entire nation... establishing an inseparable organic link between Tibet's economy and the national economy". Political and social stability and general economic development became, and still are, the foremost priorities.

Except for rare cases, a westerner arriving in Tibet today follows fixed tourist routes accompanied by a guide. As he moves from one hotel to the next, he is enchanted by the

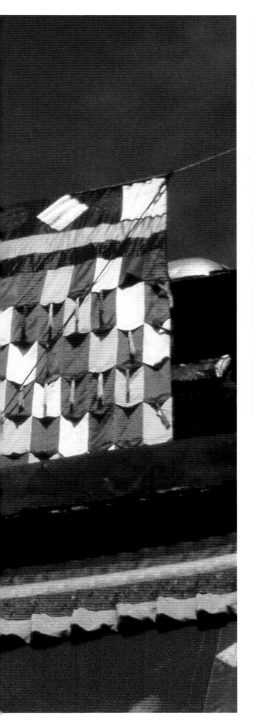

monuments and the smiles of the people but he is unable to see the reality of the country. A country in which it is even stated that "religious management departments at various levels and temple civilian management committees must guide and educate monks, nuns and followers to politically love the motherland and support the socialist system and the Communist party's leadership" (*Xizang Ribao*, 8 November 1996).

67 top Revolts and fires took place in the Jokhang square at the end of the 1980's.

67 bottom left The centre of Schöl, one of the oldest districts in Lhasa, was destroyed by bull-dozers in 1995 and replaced by the monumental Potala Square.

67 bottom right The Dalai Lama received the Nobel Peace Prize in 1989 with the recognition: "The Committee wants to emphasise the fact that the Dalai Lama in his struggle for the liberation of Tibet has opposed the use of violence. He has instead advocated peaceful solutions based upon tolerance and mutual respect in order to preserve the historical and cultural heritage of his people".

The land of snows

68 top *Tibet is unique for its exceptional altitude and ancient history. The huge plains bordered by tall mountains are home to ruins that witnessed historical events about which we have little or no knowledge.*

68 bottom *Tibet has many lakes: in the southern regions of the country they are deep with fresh water like Lake Puma Yumtsho not far from the border with Bhutan.*

"Tibet is like a house of rock that appeared from nowhere; Tibet, one of the twenty-four holy places, was the cradle of life", so says an ancient Tibetan text which finds an echo in another: "in ancient times the country was dominated by beautiful snow mountains, below there was grassland and forest, at the bottom the earth was covered by a great ocean. Time passed, the water flowed to the southern ocean, the earth emerged. The earth was covered with forests where apes, monkeys, and birds and animals dwelt happily. Then, following the law of impermanence, the trees began fewer and fewer and the earth-goddess was covered with new clothing…". The almost evolutionary concept that Tibetans have of their country runs counter to their sense of the eternal and imperturbable cosmos. Their desire for stability can be found in another song: "when the sun rises over the mountains, it shines with five colours; may changes never come and may there be prosperity". The song goes on to describe a world in which living beings are assigned their place according to the law of *karma*: the lion of the snows up on the high peaks, the antelope on the high plains, the tiger in the high forests, the wild yak among the high rocks, the vulture up on the high crags, and even the fish in the high lakes; but "may changes never come and may there be prosperity".

"A country ringed by a wall of mountains covered with snow" is one definition Tibetans give of their own country while to western minds Tibet is often considered a superbly isolated fortress, untouched by time, behind the Himalayan chain that marks the divide between the sub-continent, with its abundance of rivers, vegetation and people, and northern Asia of the bare mountains, endless and desert plains, wild animals and nomads' tents. In reality, it has been a setting for change, invasions and domination, wars, even earthquakes, and in recent times it has been shaken by political upheavals that catapulted it onto the international stage of the 20th century. Yet, to the frenetic eye of the modern traveller, remote corners of Tibet may seem unchanged in the static immensity of the desert country, an oasis outside of time.

Three black tents stand in the most protected corner of the hollow among rocks, yellow tufts of grass, stones and straw mixed with dung. Not far away, two huge yaks stand placidly while a recently born calf attempts to get to its feet. A herd of goats slowly moves over the steep slope guided by three young boys carrying catapults. In front of the tent, an old woman rhythmically shakes a whitish plastic bowl on which the faded blue words SHISHA PANGMA EXPEDITION are still legible. Soon the butter will be ready. Close by, a young

68-69 Lake Yamdrok tsho is also alpine in nature and its many branches infiltrate an intricate series of valleys. It is called the "lake in the shape of a scorpion" and plays a part in many legends. Its waters, which are not renewed by a river, are threatened by the presence of a hydro electricity plant.

69 bottom In the north of Tibet, most of the lakes contain salt-water and vary in depth. Most of them are the remains of ancient basins in the process of drying out and probably will not last for much longer. The photograph shows Lake Dangra in the heart of Chang Thang.

woman sits at a loom fixed to the ground by wooden poles. Her hand moves the bamboo shuttle back and forth pulling the coarse woollen yarn. The strip of fabric is already taking shape; once felted, it may become a cover for the boy playing with a goat horn at her side. When she sees the visitor, she stops, smiles and says something to the child who jumps up and disappears into the tent. A moment later, the boy comes out again carrying a bowl of yoghurt. Welcoming, thirst-quenching, nutritious and exquisite, yoghurt is one of Tibet's most precious foods and gifts.

This scene – except for the plastic bowl which has replaced the traditional but still common goatskin – could have been written by Sven Hedin, the great Swedish traveller who explored the world north of the Himalayas in the early 1900's. Others who could have observed the same sight are Ippolito Desideri, the adventurous Tuscan missionary who went to Tibet in the 18th century, Alessandra David Néel, the "Parisienne in Lhasa" who, dressed as a Tibetan, was the first foreigner to enter the forbidden city, or Csoma de Körös, the Hungarian scholar who reached Tibet at the start of the 19th century and was the founder of modern Tibetology. Then there were Giuseppe Tucci and Fosco Maraini, among the last to know traditional Tibet and who both described it vividly and with love. Going further back in time, we might also imagine Mongol horsemen after a day's ride across the steppes arriving at the nomad camp, uncertain whether to ransack the tents and take the women

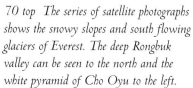

70 top The series of satellite photographs shows the snowy slopes and south flowing glaciers of Everest. The deep Rongbuk valley can be seen to the north and the white pyramid of Cho Oyu to the left.

70 centre The photographs show the entire length of the Himalayan chain as the high-level satellite tracks across Tibet. The desert lands of the north are recognisable in the picture on the left; in the centre, the heart of the ridge culminates in Mount Everest crowned with puffs of cloud; on the right, the Indian plain is hidden by the dense blanket of the summer monsoon.

70 bottom Details are much clearer when seen in photographs taken from a low-level satellite. This represents the region around Everest but now it is possible to make out the glaciers and even the moraines.

70-71 Looking south-west from above Tibet, it is clear how the Himalayas separate two very different worlds: the green countryside and rivers of Nepal and India (top) and the dry, stony plain of Tibet (bottom) in which Lake Pekutsho can be made out.

72-73 *A good stretch of the road from Shigatse to Lhatse follows the valley of the Brahmaputra through villages of farmers and animal herders. In summer the groups of houses are surrounded by fields bright green with nearly ripe barley while the enclosures are empty as this is the season that the animals graze up in the mountains.*

72 bottom *Dingri plain lies at a height of about 15,000 feet and is the first contact with Tibet for those who arrive from Nepal overland. In the rarefied air, the treeless landscape seems unreal in a setting in which even the walls of the houses, made from dried mud, are the same colour as the surrounding countryside.*

or, intimidated by the immanence of the local deities, to limit themselves to demanding food.

Separated from the rest of the world by huge mountains and existing at an altitude of between 13,000 and 16,000 feet, Tibet is the heart of Asia. An immense and inaccessible castle, tales of its marvels have filtered out over the centuries giving rise to magical and mythical stories: Tibet has become Shangri-La, the place of eternal youth where the laws of nature had been overcome and where one is in direct contact with the world of spirits - but it is also a real world with geographical, historical and human dimensions.

The Tibetan plateau is roughly 1600 miles long and 800 miles across. With the name of Xizang, today it is part of the People's Republic of China as the Autonomous Region of Tibet. It covers 471,700 square miles but the territory inhabited by people that use Tibetan language, customs and traditions is more extensive and spreads beyond the borders of the Autonomous Region: Amdo and Kham are areas that are governed by Tibetan statute within the Chinese provinces of Qinghai, Gansu, Sichuan and Yunnan while the southern Himalayan slopes inhabited by Tibetan populations, lie within India, Nepal and Bhutan.

Situated on a latitude near the Tropic of Cancer, Tibet has a dry, windy continental climate. The high altitude thins the air and reduces the oxygen content while the wind and strong evaporation lowers the humidity. Consequently the land is subjected to strong solar and cosmic radiation and to a high disparity between day and night-time temperatures. Some areas, like Lhasa, enjoy a relatively mild climate with temperatures ranging from −10°C in winter to +20°C in summer, but there are peripheral areas where in winter the thermometer drops to -40°C, rising in summer barely above 0°. This results in the subsoil being

73 top, 73 centre, 73 bottom Despite the inhospitable terrain of Dingri plain, it is an area with a rich historical and cultural past where ruined castles and forts are evidence of the former existence of ruling families and garrisons. Many of the smaller forts date from the time of the invasion of the Gurkhas, the Nepalese soldiers that attempted to penetrate Tibet at the end of the 18th century but who were forced back.

74-75 Purang is an important city in west Tibet. It is a farming centre but, more importantly, a trading centre that stands on a tributary of the Ganges on the road that descends towards the border with India. Purang is also much visited by Indian merchants who know the town as Taklakot.

76 top In the valleys where the land is fairly flat and irrigable, the fields look like squares separated by water channels lined with bushes and trees. Barley, in particular, grows at an altitude of 12,000 feet and is the basic food for Tibetans.

76 centre In summer the bushes and conifers of the meadows preside over a carpet of flowers in Kham where rainfall is more abundant. Seen against the alpine background of rocky mountains and streams, the views are very pleasant.

76 bottom As one moves east, rainfall levels increase. The other large region in east Tibet, Amdo, today part of the province of Qinghai, is also relatively blessed with water sources that create large meadows where shepherds on horseback lead their numerous flocks to feed.

77 top The inhabitants of Kham are both shepherds and monks who, as is common, have their monastery set high on a ridge. The monastery of Garsi seems to hang on a picturesque slope above the houses of the civilian population.

permanently frozen. The phenomenon is common in peri-arctic regions and is known as *permafrost*. The hardness and impermeability of the ground below the thin surface layer prevents water from penetrating so that when the few rain-showers fall, they create short-lived swamps.

Rainfall is relatively abundant in the eastern regions of Tibet but is scarce in the west of the country and in the area immediately north of the Himalayas, as the mountains form an almost impassable barrier. The few summer clouds to cross the mountains are the remnants of monsoon storms from the Indian Ocean that have just brought rain to the sub-continent. The storms that they bring are sudden and violent. Set against a perennially blue sky, they are tall masses of dark clouds run through by darting thunderbolts and joined to the ground by a whitish curtain of rain and hail.

If the summer brings short, violent rainstorms, the dominant weather feature from winter until the return of the monsoon is the implacable wind that scourges everything in its path and raises stinging clouds of sand. In the lower areas the vegetation helps to create the basis for life but almost everywhere there are only sparse tufts of grass half-covered by sand and stones. As soon as the rain falls in summer, however, everything suddenly bursts into life; the grass turns green again, small flowers of all colours appear, the slopes are covered with a thousand different hues and the tops of the mountains are covered with fresh snow. It is a beautiful setting described in an ancient prophecy as the land in which "the tall mountains are the pillars that hold up the sky" and "they sparkle like

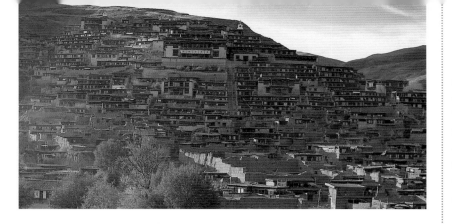

76-77 *Proud in his saddle protected by a yak blanket, the sleeve of his* chupa *lowered below his shoulder and his whip in hand, the nomad moves across the meadows as the lord of his world. Although roads are beginning to reach many areas of Tibet and the number of vehicles is increasing, the horse is still the most common means of transport.*

78 top, 78 centre Much drier than the eastern territories, central-western Tibet is really just a high altitude desert. Water is scarce but when present, it is destructive. Instead of making the land fertile, it washes the topsoil away and accumulates in mud-filled torrents around which the herds find little food.

stupa of white crystal"; lower down, "the ochre slopes are like mountains of gold, there are incense plants of pleasant scent, autumn is coloured with golden flowers, and summer is coloured with turquoise flowers".

The masses of snow on the peaks of the mountains form a reservoir of water that ensures the continuity of life as they slowly melt. Water is sacred down on the plateau; springs are the homes of underground spirits, the gift of the gods or the legacy left by holy men that made them bubble up for the benefit of all living beings. Springs are valuable assets that must not be contaminated but looked after with all due care and attention.

Winter is the dry season. The sun shines high in the sky producing enough warmth, despite the coldness of the air, for creatures to recover their energy levels after the terrible freeze of the previous night. Blades of grass, despite being dry and yellowed, still manage to appear to provide fodder for the yaks, sheep, horses, wild donkeys, gazelles and, consequently, for wolves and man too. Things change when the Great Snows fall on the highlands. It is a rare but recurrent phenomenon that threatens the economy and life of the nomads at a single blow.

The sky is a medley of dark and light grey stains. Swirls of sleet are gusted by the wind raising the crests of an endless pearly sea higher and higher. A group of tents emerges against the white blanket, dark shreds of material encrusted with ice from which a thin plume of smoke rises. Inside, the hearth is a sheet of translucent ice with a red flame flickering at its centre. The subdued cry of a child is heard in the background mingled with the gentle voice of the mother as she wraps her baby in her furs and tries to breastfeed it.

"We have nothing left, we have no more food, the yaks have been scattered, and perhaps are dead..." explains the man in a broken voice as he welcomes the members of an emergency aid expedition.

In recent years, great falls of snow have occurred for almost two consecutive years. There were seventeen falls during the 1997-98 winter and 6 feet of snow fell in one night destroying the economy of even the strongest. Usually, several years pass between one disaster and the next, giving people time to recover.

"The other time was sixty years ago", tells the head-man of a village north of Nagchu in northern Tibet, "I was a child but I remember it well. The snow arrived unexpectedly in the night and covered everything. It was cold, so cold that people died whilst on the move, without realising. I can see

78-79 *The presence of the river was the determining factor in the birth of the Tibetan civilization. Shigatse, a major administrative centre and Tibet's second largest city, stands on the banks of the Brahmaputra connected to Lhasa by a highway that follows the course of the river. In the foreground of the photograph we see the traditional quarters of Tashilhunpo, the monastic city of the Panchen Lama, while the modern city stretches almost out of view in the background.*

79 top, 79 centre *The long, hard work of channelling and directing mountain streams is rewarded by the creation of fields and, subsequently, villages.*

79 bottom *During the rainy season, the mountain streams that descend the slopes of the Himalayas are particularly powerful before they reach the villages.*

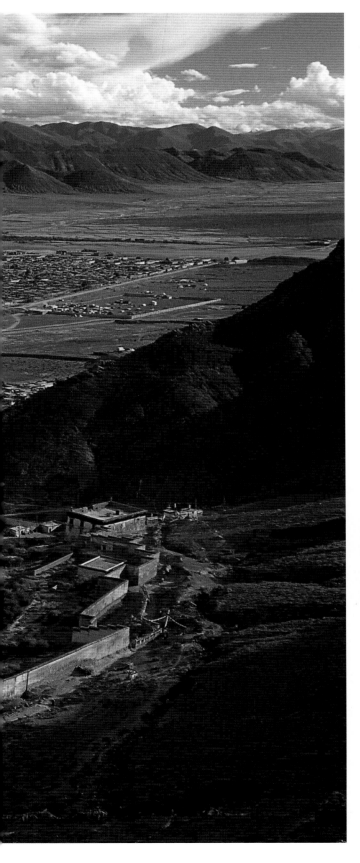

80 top Tibet in winter is a unique experience. Sandstorms often blow in the dry western regions while, in the east, the snow transforms the countryside into a frozen and desolate landscape.

80-81 Glaciers and snow dominate the views. This is Amdo beside the river Gar Chu that flows into the Yellow River. On the left, a row of chorten *marks a ceremonial route followed by pilgrims and devotees.*

80 bottom, 81 top If the snow is too thick or the bad weather lasts too long, both wild and domesticated grass-eating animals are unable to reach the little vegetation below even by scraping the snow away with their hooves and horns. Exceptionally deep snowfalls that sometimes occur in the western regions can create serious problems of survival.

81 bottom Snow sometimes also falls in the region of Lhasa. This is Mila pass, to the east of the capital, during winter.

them, the inhabitants of my village, on the morning they decided to go and look for the yaks up on the mountain in the snow. The cold paralysed them as they walked or rode. In spring, when the sun melted the snow, their shadows protected the frozen "pedestals" on which they stood. They looked like a ghost army..."

The landscape over which the stream of physical and human events passes seems eternal but the plateau has its own story, one of titanic cataclysms, still partly in progress, over geological eras that can only be read and interpreted on their own timescale.

According to the universally accepted tectonic plate theory, when Pangaea (the original land mass) broke up, the continental plates began to drift away from one another. The land that now corresponds to Tibet remained part of the Siberian block that was in turn bounded to the south by Tethys, a vast sea in which huge layers of sediment accumulated on the ocean floor over hundreds of millions of years. Meanwhile, after being detached from the African land mass, the Indian plate slowly but inevitably travelled up from the south until it began to press up against the Siberian plate. At the end of the Eocene epoch, roughly forty million years ago, the bed of Tethys began to compress, fold, and curl over under the pressure into a series of parallel crests that divided the ocean into two smaller seas. The continual movement and pressure grew. All the rocks that had accumulated on the sea bed were crushed, folded, fractured and forced to slide up against one another. The movement continued and the contorted rock layers with their fossil remains were pushed upwards during the Miocene epoch roughly fifteen million years ago. The layers formed immense folds that rose and then began to bend southwards, distorting the previous landscape. Set

82-83 The 26,000 foot Shisha Pangma has large glaciers but as they are not steep, the mountain is considered "easy" and is a favourite destination of climbing expeditions. The base camp can easily be reached by road.

is still continuing. Recent calculations have shown that the Himalayan chain has risen a further 3900 feet since the Pliocene epoch and 975 feet over the last ten thousand years.

The chain of the Nyenchen Tanglha marks the watershed between the catchment basin that drains into the Indian Ocean and that from where the water flows down— if it flows down— towards the China seas. This chain also forms an anthropographical barrier: to the south is the "liveable" world with rivers, villages, fields and roads while to the north lies the Chang Thang which appears as soon as one passes the watershed. It is a sea of crests, all different yet similar and uniform, which stretches as far as the horizon and way beyond.

The Chang Thang covers almost five-sevenths of the entire Tibetan plateau. It is bounded to the south by the Nyenchen Tanglha and to the north by the steep Kunlun chain which, in turn, forms the boundary of the Taklimakan desert and Sinkiang. The waters of the Chang Thang are mostly unable to flow out so that the little water that falls is collected in large basins that have no outlet. The basins are the remains of ancient ocean beds in the stage of drying out. The flat blue line that marks stagnant winter water is surrounded by a white strip of sparkling salt crystals that gets absorbed by the brackish water when the rains fall while all around the land is bare. Melting snow feeds the water-flats but, when this ceases, the land dries out giving rise to salt-flats which have traditionally provided work and life to the nomads. In an interview with the

82 bottom Kang Pongchen is at the peak at the end of the Shisha Pangma chain before it slopes down towards Lake Pekutsho where its waters flow. In a treeless environment, the glaciers flow right down to the uninterrupted, stony, high altitude desert. This is the wide and arid Porong valley that is only inhabited by nomads.

83 top Shisha Pangma, seen from the road that descends from Tong la to Dingri, overlooks the Porong valley where the Phung Chu river has its source. The river crosses much of southern Tibet and enters Nepal where it is known as the Arun, a fast-flowing tributary of the Ganges.

83 bottom Karo la is the name of the pass crossed by the road from Lhasa to Gyantse. For centuries this was the only road between the two cities and the only means of access for the first western expeditions leaving from Sikkim or Bhutan. Living next to the glaciers that descend almost to the edge of the road are groups of nomads by now accustomed to lorries, cars and inquisitive cameras.

against the background of the geological timescale, it was a cataclysmic event. This was the birth of the Himalaya mountain range which, together with the Karakorum, Caucasus and the Alps, was changing the face of the globe. As a result of the implacable force from the south, the edge of the sub-continent began to slide below that of the northern plate which forced upwards. It was a slow, gradual but unremitting movement. The sea disappeared completely and the land surface was raised by a height of 13,000 feet taking the peaks of the 6,500 feet mountains that had cut Tethys in two to a total altitude of 19,500 feet. This was the formation of the massive mountain range called the Trans Himalaya — to use the expression of Sven Hedin and the first western travellers who saw them — or Nyenchen Tanglha in the Tibetan language. Behind the mountains stretches the Chang Thang or Northern Plain. The movement of the land masses

84 top and 84 centre Even the Chang Thang becomes slowly less arduous as one moves eastwards. The brief summer rains transform the landscape into flower-filled meadows which lift the spirits and guarantee food for both domestic and wild animals.

84 bottom For the rest of the year, the Chang Thang is nothing but an infinite expanse of stones that provide a solid grip for the tyres of off-road vehicles. During the short season of the rains, the water does not penetrate the subsoil due to an impermeable layer of frozen earth and the steppes are turned into a bog.

anthropologist Melvyn Goldstein, a salt-collector described his work: "On the trip to the lake we go very leisurely so that our animals can maintain their strenght. Pasture is a problem... since there are so many nomads and animals concentrated there. Because of this, we send an advance team of four or five men to dig up and pack the salt. Then when we arrive with the animals, we can load up immediately and leave the next day". A great number of wild animals live around the few freshwater springs and short watercourses – yaks, horses and donkeys, gazelles, rabbits and wolves – but, moving south, these slowly give way to herds of domestic animals and the men that own them.

The eastern side of the Chang Thang is not closed off by mountains. Here the land slowly slopes down towards Qinghai, the huge Chinese province that incorporates the region traditionally called Amdo largely inhabited by Tibetans. Here lies the large Lake Kokonor and, near one of the tributaries of the Yellow River, the Amnye Machen mountain chain where one of the Tibetan people's most sacred mountains rises. The Tangula chain runs east-west and separates Qinghai from the Autonomous Region of Tibet.

The Karakorum range marks the western boundary of the Chang Thang. Here the Nyenchen Tanglha chain becomes the Kailash range which includes the sub-continent's holy mountain par excellence. Under the name of Kangdise, Kailash, Meru, Kang Rinpoche and Axis of the World, it is worshipped by Buddhists, Hindus and Jainists. The four rivers that have brought life to great

84-85 Numerous ancient lakes in Chang Thang have been turned into salt flats. If the material is rock salt, the merchants load it up and take it away but often it is of different types of salts most of which are unusable and prevent all life from growing in the soil.

85 top The inhabitants of Chang Thang are nomadic herdsmen of goats, yak and sheep. Animals are their source of wealth and make them almost autonomous within the limits of their own survival economy.

85 bottom There are still many wild animals in the Chang Thang such as hares, gazelles, wolves, yak and kyang or wild donkeys.

The land of snows 85

86 top *Rains can sometimes be abundant during the summer when the banks of the Brahmaputra will overflow and the water invade fields and tree plantations.*

86-87 *Floods submerge the trees and force livestock to be transferred through the muddy water. For humans, it is often a time of famine.*

civilizations have their origin on and around this mountain. To the north is the Indus which first flows northwards, crosses the Tibetan province of Ngari, then Ladakh and eventually enters Pakistan. The Karakorum chain forces the river to deviate south where it begins to widen as it heads towards the Indian Ocean near Karachi. The Indus valley was home to great and advanced civilizations; it was here that the world of the ancient Greeks came into contact with the civilization of India, that Herodotus found the inspiration for his tales, that the armies of Alexander the Great passed and that St. Thomas succeeded in converting king Gondophemes, if the apocryphal Acts are to be

believed. The second of the four great rivers, not so well-known in the west, is the Sutlej that flows into the Indus; the Sutlej valley was once the site of Kyunglung Ngulkar, a capital of the ancient kingdom of Shang Shung. The third river is the Karnali, one of the rivers that descends from "the hair of Shiva" (the glaciers that are the sources of the waters that unite to form the Ganges, the holy river that creates the basis of life for much of India's population). The fourth river is the Brahmaputra which is called the Tsangpo Chenpo (Great River) in Tibet and is marked on the maps as Yarlung Tsangpo. It is the river that gave rise to the Tibetan civilization. It flows down a fault line parallel to the Himalayas that was formed where the folds turn south. Its valley is closed on the north side by the Nyenchen Tanglha chain and to the south by the Himalayas as far as the eastern end of the country where the river meets the Namcha Barwa, a 23,000

88 top *In summer 1998, an exceptional flood submerged not just the trees but also the sand dunes so raising the level of the water. The only benefit to be had from the situation was the little navigation that takes place on the river.*

88 centre *Traditional boats made from treated and sewn yak skins are still in use on the Brahmaputra. For centuries the light, practical boats were the only means of crossing rivers.*

88 bottom *This aerial photograph shows the river in full flood. The valley is covered with water from one side to the other, fields and villages are flooded and crops destroyed. In the area around Gonkhar, 53 people died and a state of emergency was declared.*

foot mountain covered in ice. To round the mountain, it has dug out an extraordinary gorge at the mountain base, a full 16,000 feet lower than the tip of the mountain. The gorge is a magical place: for geologists, for whom the rock layers are a treasure trove, for botanists, who can explore flora ranging from a rain forest to alpine meadows, and for the pilgrim who plunges into the sacred Beyul Pemakhö, the Hidden Valley of Flowers. The Brahmaputra curves almost 300° around the Namcha Barwa so that it can flow majestically southwards to mix with the waters of the Ganges and out through the delta into the Gulf of Bengal.

The other rivers in southern Tibet are of modest size but flow fast through deep gorges and ravines. As the Himalayas rose, the waters from the northern land mass that flowed south began to dig out passages in the growing barrier. These rivers are hemmed in on either side by 23-26,000 foot high mountains and played a fundamental role as means of communication between the Indian plain and the lands north of the Himalayas.

The ancient roads towards the west follow some of the tributaries of the Ganges. One of these, now closed, crosses the Himalayan chain below Mount Kamet, a 23,000 foot mountain on the border between Tibet and India, and runs down towards Badrinath, a holy place for the Hindus and one of the most venerated sources of the Ganges. Another road – occasionally opened to adventurous tourists – follows the course of the Karnali river and passes by the slopes of Mount Gurla Mandhata near to the river's sources. At 25,116 feet, the Gurla Mandhata is the highest mountain in Tibet's most sacred area, the territory surrounding Mount Kailash, and the splendour of its ice is reflected in the blue waters of Lake Manosarovar. The road that follows the course of the Trisuli is also closed but for centuries it was a preferred means of transit between China and India. A reminder of the road's role can be seen in an inscription carved in the rock to the north of the town of Dzongkha, the capital of the ancient kingdom of Gunthang. After study by Tibetan and Chinese experts, it was deciphered as "here passed a delegation in the sixth month of the second year of Xian qing", which date corresponds to 675 AD. Dzongkha was one of the most frequently used routes by Indian and Tibetan grand masters on trips between the two countries and it is said that this was the route followed by Padmasambhava when he came to Tibet for the

88-89 Flat-bottomed ferries with motors, similar to barges, are mainly used to cross the river today. The ferries wait until they are filled with people and goods before starting the crossing that takes just over an hour.

89 bottom Monks and pilgrims on their way to Samye also cross the Brahmaputra on the ferry. Their great faith will have sustained them on their long journeys either on foot or by cadging rides in lorries; now they are nearly at their destination.

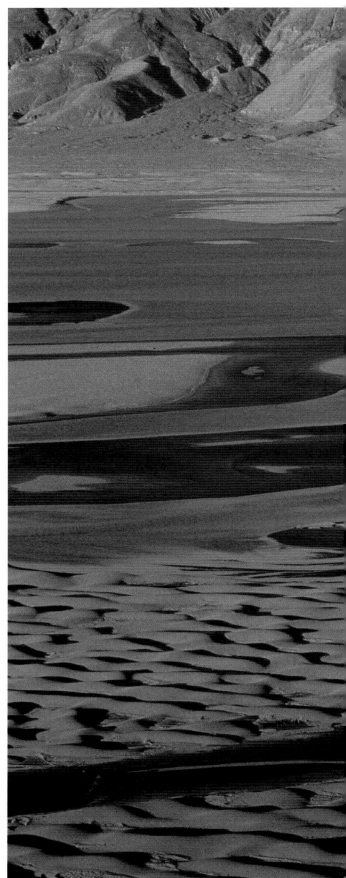

90 top *The Brahmaputra seems to have played with the sand creating a composition of elegant dunes constantly transformed by the wind.*

90 centre *The water also seems playful along the shores of Lake Yamdrog, the beauty of which is heightened by the total absence of buildings or man.*

90-91 *Where the valley widens and the slope is reduced, the slow drift of the water creates whirls between sandy islands which seem to rise and sink depending on the level of the water.*

foundation of the monastery of Samye and by Milarepa, the great Tibetan mystic and poet of the 11th century. Milarepa stopped there at length and praised the beauty of the air, the mountains and the waters of this enchanting valley in his One Hundred Thousand Songs.

Tourists know better the passage that follows the course of the Bhote Kosi. This river has its source in the bright, dry and frozen valley of the highlands and flows for just a few miles (two of which are vertical) into the hot and dense world of the land of the monsoons. It runs through ravines gouged between steep rock-walls that are gradually covered in thicker vegetation and crossed by precarious bridges. The narrow and often blocked road that connects the bridges might be considered a masterpiece of road-building in its own way. It is one of the few official means of communication between Nepal and Tibet and, in addition to the tourist traffic, is a main route for trucks importing and exporting consumer goods. Zhangmu (Dram to the Tibetans) is a "vertical" town: it falls 600 feet from the first huts at the top of the town to the Customs gate at the bottom. A narrow road winds down the steep hill in a series of U-turns flanked on either side by a row of tall, slender houses. This town is home to merchants, drivers, smugglers,

prostitutes and the military. Suffocating the small shops selling knick-knacks, lorries with Chinese inscriptions hug the walls exchanging goods with lorries bearing Nepalese number plates. If it rains, their wheels get stuck in the mud, the lorries begin to slide and the traffic stops just like when a landslide bloks the route. The remaining vehicles shuttle to and fro in the section of road still free while people revert to walking and goods are hefted onto bearers' shoulders.

Another river is the Phung Chu that springs from the base of the Shisha Pangma in the Porong plain. It first flows eastwards then turns south, collecting the waters that flow from the north slopes of Everest and Makalu, and hurls itself through sheer ravines towards Nepal where it takes the name Arun. Its banks are lined with forts and

90 bottom and 91 bottom In some places along the Brahmaputra, the sand carried by the wind accumulates in strange places and is even deposited close to the tops of the mountains. These views are typical of the area between Gonkhar, where the airport is, and Tsethang.

92-93 At only 11,000 feet, the Yarlung valley is a fertile, easily irrigable zone south of Tsethang that is generally believed to have been the cradle of the Tibetan civilization. In the arid and difficult terrain of Tibet, the trees that grow here are a valuable asset.

92 bottom The solid-looking houses in the Yarlung valley are built using the traditional method of stones and mud bricks with small windows. In a country where glass was not known, this was the only method of giving protection from the cold.

first Italians, with Giuseppe Tucci, to follow this route; in his book, *Secret Tibet*, he describes the force of the river Tista.

"…everywhere there are waterfalls, torrents, whirlpools and springs; you have the sensation that these mountains are still amazingly young, that the process of levelling is in full course, that everything is falling, rushing, flowing, crumbling; the water carries away huge quantities of soil and sand and rolls down boulders of all sizes, destroying the giants day by day".

Once over the pass, the traveller was confronted by the Chumby Valley. In its unknown, rarefied and transparent atmosphere, one discovered the harsh and desolate highland dominated by Chomolari, the majestic and isolated 23,000 foot mountain that sparkles with ice like the tip of a diamond.

The rivers, valleys and mountains of the Himalayas are in continual evolution but, from an aeroplane, look like a gigantic petrified sea. The chains of mountains follow one another like series of parallel wrinkles — brown, bare, immobile waves marked on the top by a thin white line. Then, little by little, the snow gradually increases, the slopes are tinged with green and one can make out the shape of a tree. Large moraines enclosing small lakes and glaciers appear, separated by crests, spurs and walls until there, in the distance, one sees the majestic, thrilling and superb mountains rising to 26,000 feet and more.

To the east stands the Kanchendzonga, the third

93 top Although exploited by an ancient and well-organised irrigation system, the water courses are difficult to control. While they are often dry, the wide beds are created during periods of heavy rains when the torrents can become very dangerous.

93 centre, 93 bottom The origins of farming in the Yarlung valley go back so far they are lost in myths. The houses stand between fertile fields, the trees line the irrigation channels and roads and paths facilitate movement. Compared to the lands of the nomads where living conditions are far harder, this seems an area blessed by the gods.

94-95 At the end of its passage through Tibet, the swirling Brahmaputra passes over the large mountain chain through ravines dug out over the millennia. The river passes through one of the deepest gorges in the world which contains a range of vegetation from glacial tundra to a luxuriant rain forest.

trenches associated with the Gurkha invasion during the 18th century; other ruins are older but are just as mysterious as the many caverns, tombs and sections of wall to be found along the valley. A recent carbon 14 test dates one to around the year 1000 AD. It might be the remains of one of the small kingdoms the Tibetan empire broke into, it might be …

Further east, the next large river is the Tista which collects the waters from Sikkim and takes them to the Ganges. Its valley was described in detail and enthusiasm by explorers entering Tibet at the beginning of the 20th century. The caravans marched north from Darjeeling or Gantok for days along paths that rise from the rain-forest to the pass that took them into Tibet. The descriptions of the country in the travel journals of these explorers positively burst with life. Maraini was one of the

96 top In a "vertical" land, mountain streams gouge deep beds from the ground and form powerful whirlpools where they join a main river. This is often where villages are built due to the presence of water and the loosened terrain.

96 bottom Thermal waters are not rare in Tibet. Called chu tsen, they are often situated in unpopulated areas and cannot be used for therapeutic purposes. The photograph shows the formation of a hot water pool along the lower reaches of the Brahmaputra.

highest mountain on earth and considered one of the most difficult by mountaineers. It stands on the border between Nepal and Sikkim in an area that has been inhabited by Tibetans for centuries and that has both Tibetan miths and history. As the eastern outpost, it is exposed to the fury of the monsoons that blow off the Gulf of Bengal and is mantled by a thick blanket of ice and snow. It is surrounded by the Beyul Demojong, the Hidden Valley of Rice. The literal translation of Kanchendzonga is the "Mountain of the Five Treasures" in which the treasures refer to barley, corn, maize, millet and the potato. The last was only recently added to the holy sequence and it can demonstrate, perhaps, how strong the forces of tradition still are. There is a prophecy that the treasures hidden there "will be opened at the end of time".

Further to the west rises the Makalu, the "Great Black". This is the fifth highest mountain on earth and is a harsh and difficult but fascinating challenge to climbers. Geologically it is a mass of granite that was thrust up amongst the schists during the

96-97 At this stage, the Brahmaputra flows at low altitude through luxuriant forests. The clearings, probably obtained by slash and burn techniques, are used to cultivate millet. The environment and conditions of life here are similar to those found on the southern slopes of the Himalaya.

Miocene epoch. Being more resistant than the shale, it was laid bare by the elements over the millennia until it formed an almost perfect pyramidal shape sprinkled with snow and ice. A blend of white, pink and dark, gleaming or speckled with bluish shadows, at every hour of the day, the Makalu looks like a brilliant jewel in a crown of lower mountains. In Tibetan cosmogony, the Makalu is set in the centre of the Beyul Khenbalung, the Hidden Valley of Artemisiae.

The highest and most imposing, but perhaps not the most beautiful, is Mount Everest which hides behind the massive spurs of Lhotse (south peak),

Nuptse (west peak) and Shartse (east peak). The immense bastion of dark and yellowish rock is nearly all covered by ice and snow. It is separated from Lhotse by the South Col, a perennially windswept saddle 26,000 feet high that has been the spectacular and dramatic setting of many mountaineering tragedies. On the north side, where the mountain's outposts are lower, Everest's north wall dominates the valley of Dzakar chu, the River of the White Stones, in which Rongbuk, one of the highest monasteries in the world, is situated at 16,000 feet.

Not far from Everest stands Cho Oyu, the

97 bottom Namcha Barwa is a mountain of about 23,000 feet covered with huge glaciers that lies only 17 miles from Gyala Peltri, another mountain of the same height. The Brahmaputra passes between the two at a height of only 7,000 feet.

98 *The valley created by the Bhote Kosi river falls from the desert at an altitude of 16,000 feet to the dense Nepalese forests in just a few miles distance. To descend the valley by road, you have to execute a seemingly endless number of hairpin turns.*

99 top left *The edge of the road either looks over deep ravines or passes below massive walls of rock. Although continuously looked after, this road is often blocked by landslides that either cover the road or unexpectedly carry some of it away.*

mountain of the Sacred Turquoise. It was one of the first mountains over 26,000 feet to be climbed and its Tibetan side is still the destination of many expeditions that want the glory of scaling such a high mountain but at relatively minor risk. It is a jewel that shimmers with snow and stands out among the high, snow-capped peaks that enclose the south side of the Dingri plateau.

The Shisha Pangma stands entirely on Tibetan soil. Its snow-laden chain rises huge above the barren plain of Porong fed by the glacier waters of the Pekutsho salt basin. The Shisha Pangma is also over 26,000 feet high and a popular destination for mountaineering expeditions as it is one of the relatively easy climbs. Its name, only recently conferred on the mountain, literally means "flesh of the dead and land of swamps" and refers to the type of soil found at its feet; its ancient name, Phola Gonchen, which is still in use among local communities and refers to the ancestral divinity of the territory, predates the advent of Buddhism and the history of Tibet itself.

99 top right, 99 centre *As one descends the slopes in summer, the limpid air is slowly replaced by the mists of the monsoon and the baked earth becomes covered by bushes, trees and finally forests.*

99 bottom *Zhagmu, the border town, stands at 7,000 feet in the middle of a forest. The continuous traffic is responsible for the town's abnormal vertical layout on land which, unfortunately, is often subject to landslides.*

100 top On the flowery meadows of Kama chu opposite Chomolonzo there stands an impressive Tibetan tent. This is a rare event, probably to do with some trekking or climbing expedition, as for most of the year this valley is deserted and in summer is exclusively inhabited by nomads.

100-101 The north walls of Makalu and Chomolonzo are reflected in the lake below the Pass of Langma la. Further down there is the Karma chu valley which begins below the east wall of Everest and opens into the river Arun. This wild and deserted valley is filled with alpine flowers and may still be inhabited by the snow leopard.

101 top Rongbuk valley is closed off by Mount Everest at its head. A series of frozen channels adds to the spectacular landscape.

101 centre Photographed with a powerful telescopic lens, Cho Oyu seems to dominate the town of old Dingri. In fact, there is still a long way to go to reach the "Mountain of the Sacred Turquoise".

101 bottom Mount Kailash in west Tibet is only 20,000 feet high but is certainly one of the country's most famous mountains. Sacred mountain par excellence, it has never been climbed and its snow has never seen the footprint of man.

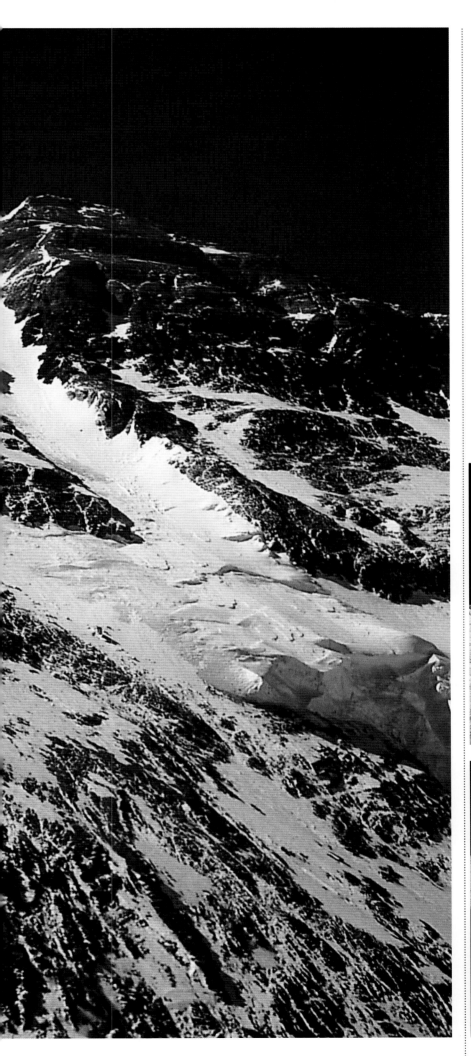

102 top The soaring, elegant north wall of Everest was the objective of the first English expeditions whose goal was to reach the summit. They would arrive from Sikkim on foot or horseback and only see the mountain after months of travel. Of those climbers, Mallory was perhaps the first to reach the top, but he died among the ices taking his secret with him.

102-103, 103 bottom The summit of Everest seen from the North Col looks like a mass of dark rocks and ice slips. Less wild seen from afar, Everest was always venerated and respected by the monks of Rongbuk monastery and by the local population: it was considered the seat of the gods and should be off limits. Despite their wish that the mountain should remain sacred, during the last years Everest has been opened to the western world and access to the summit has become a commercial and competitive enterprise.

103 top Cho Oyu is another massive mountain over 26,000 feet high that stands just 17 miles from Everest. The mass of snow-covered rocks was observed with interest by Shipton's 1921 English expedition which was studying the country for a way to climb Everest.

103 centre The Gran Couloir is a traditional way to climb Everest from the north. Every year the number of expeditions from all over the world wishing to reach the top via this route increases. The often uncertain conditions of the weather, the danger of avalanches and the problems related to the altitude make the climb dangerous and, considering the number of victims, one might think that the Rongbuk monks were right.

104-105 The rising sun shines gold on the east wall of Everest and Lhotse, the two peaks separated by the South Col. The east wall, known as Kangshung, is perhaps the most spectacular view of the great mountain.

Life in Tibet:

nomads, farmers, merchants
... and cadres

106 top Nomads are without doubt some of the Tibetans that most fascinate the western world. The inhabitants of central Asia evoke the magic of a life of freedom lived in unrestricted spaces whereas their lives are in fact extremely hard.

106 centre The nomad economy used to be, and in many cases still is, one of self-sufficiency achieved by exchanging assets with farmers. The family has to build the tent, look after the animals, prepare the food, weave and sew clothes. Looms are used to prepare wool and weave fabrics that can be used for bartering.

106 bottom The animals are tied in a line when it is time for milking. The dry and rocky land allows only a small quantity of milk to be produced which is then turned into butter and yoghurt, the nomads' most important and valuable food-type.

While the visitor's gaze wanders bewildered around the bleak mountains that line the river Brahmaputra as the little bus travels from the airport into Lhasa, the Tibetan guide suddenly raises his voice to describe the three categories of Tibetans: the nomads and their livestock that live dispersed far and wide around the country, the farmers who work in the fields and live in villages, and the merchants that travel and deal and who mainly live in the cities. This is a classic picture that corresponds to the reality that every tourist expects to find on arrival in Tibet. It should be added that the possibility of meeting nomads in their own environment is limited to sporadic occasions on some carriageable pass where they have become accustomed to being photographed by

106-107 The wealth of a nomad family is measured by its animals: Tibetans call herds of sheep and goats the "white" and droves of yak the "black". In past times, well-off families might have owned one thousand "black" and an unspecified number of "white".

107 bottom right and left Children learn to ride from an early age. From high up on the horse, they begin to feel proud of belonging to a people that "need not bow down to the earth" to live. This pride is typical of nomads and increases with age.

crowds of foreigners.

Tibetan nomads might be included among those "wandering herdsmen of central Asia", to use the expression of the poet Giacomo Leopardi, that conjure up a majestic and harsh world and represent the romantic idea of the impossible and of the dream. Such a world is far from the reality of western life. In fact Tibetan nomads, *drogpa*, mostly live on the freezing windy steppes of Chang Thang at a height of 13,000-16,000 feet. They are one of the peoples of the world who live in the most arduous of conditions.

The first problem encountered when living in the highlands is physical. The human body first has to cope with the problems caused by the altitude. As is

well-known, the atmosphere thins as the altitude increases. At 13,000 feet, the atmospheric pressure is more or less halved and consequently the availability of oxygen. To ensure the body cells receive enough oxygen, the organism has to increase the number of oxygen transporters, i.e. red blood cells, and force the heart to work harder. Next, the increase in solar radiation damages and dehydrates the skin and injures the eyes by causing lesions of the cornea. Finally, the intense, cold wind and wide temperature range force the blood capillaries to make continuous adaptations. In such conditions, survival is only granted by perfect acclimatization and phenomenal physical strength, the result of a long and fierce process of natural selection.

There are few nomads in Tibet but the territory over which they range is vast. Despite being widely scattered, their society has precise and indispensable rules that enabled their forefathers to divide up grazing land successfully and to help one another. Different authorities have passed over their heads through the centuries: the kingdom of Shang Shung, the Tibetan empire, various local nobles and the many Dalai Lamas. The individuals to whom they pay taxes and tributes and to whom they turn in times of disaster may have changed but their way of life, dictated by the primary needs of existence, remained the same; likewise their faith, with its various creeds, which maintained intact their profound veneration of the spirits that govern the forces of nature. Only in the last few years their customs have begun to suffer radical changes, since the creation of the Autonomous Region of Tibet and the arrival of the wind of modernity that reaches even the remotest regions.

Nomadic society is based on the family, sometimes polygamic, that forms an almost self-sufficient entity able to provide for its different needs. Old people are respected and honoured and final decisions are taken by the father. The mother is

108 top left, 108 top right Most Tibetan nomads live in the Chang Thang north of the Brahmaputra but they also use land in the southern valleys above the agricultural fields. Here the children learn to wear the traditional dress with the beautiful silver buckle when they are still young.

108 centre, 108 bottom right Throughout Tibet the children are suckled until they are two, perhaps three years old unless a younger sibling comes along. This helps to protect the youngsters from illnesses and allows their stomachs to cope better with the rather basic food when they are old enough to digest it.

108 bottom left Expeditions and tourists on their way to the base camp north of Everest are transported by lorry or jeep along a road that passes through the Dzakar valley. Local people, unable to afford motorized vehicles, still use traditional carts though fitted with modern wheels.

109 Exposed to strong solar radiation, the skin of nomads' faces is heavily wrinkled. In order to protect themselves they often use felt hats and smear butter on their faces.

at high altitude, yaks suffer the heat and rarely survive below 13,000 feet.

Nomads used to live in groups in tents while their innumerable grazing animals wandered around this small society but today they are rapidly becoming settled and tents are being replaced by simple stone buildings in which the families spend the coldest months. The herds of yak represent nomad wealth and are called "the black", in contrast to "the white" which refers to goats and sheep. The "yak" is actually the term for the castrated male animal used as a beast of burden while the females are called *dri* and make up most of the grazing animals; uncastrated males, *pho*, live up on the mountains and are only brought down when there are females on heat. Nonetheless, the western term "yak" is used to indicate the whole species and Tibetans burst into laughter when they hear the term "yak butter". So as not to accumulate too much bad *karma*, nomads do not kill their animals but try to circumvent the problem by getting someone from the "impure" caste to do it according to tradition or by asking some wretch who is prepared to take on the "sin". The insides of the

responsible for maintaining relations with neighbouring families and above all for guiding marriage policy. She also weaves and prepares the *chupa*, the traditional clothes, both for men and for women; she manages the family's economy and decides how and when the various jobs are carried out. Children are loved and appreciated but fundamentally they must obey; they carry the water, collect yak dung and put it to dry, and even when still young are sent to watch over distant herds. The tents are made from woven and felted yak wool and contain all the household chattels, the altar with its ritual objects and the hearth. The diet of the nomads is made up of *tsampa* (toasted barley flour bought from farmers), milk, yoghurt and meat. In the life of the nomad, the yak is the primary source of food and the lynch-pin of the economy.

Strong, robust and with long hair to protect it from every kind of bad weather, the yak was domesticated by man in ancient times. Its milk is thick, creamy and rich in fats; its meat is nutritious and tasty; its skin is used to prepare leather bags, bedding and boats; its wool is woven into blankets and tent covers while its bones are the raw material for furniture and pendants. Adapted perfectly to life

110 The Dzakar chu valley is shared with the nomads by farmers who live in the lower, more fertile areas irrigated by the river. This is also the area of the samadrog, i.e. the families that base their living on a mixed economy, for example, farming and grazing.

111 top and centre right The people in this region are still linked to ancient customs; not only do they still wear the chupa, the traditional dress that is different for men and women, but they also love to wear jewellery. The rich might wear gold and turquoise earrings but most have to be content with turquoise and coral tied with a thread.

111 centre left Amber necklaces with large rough pearls and necklaces with zi, a hard stone found particularly beneficial, are common. The more "eyes" they have, the more they are worth. Imitations are frequent as an authentic zi may cost a fortune. Jewellery is part of a family's wealth and forms a woman's dowry.

111 bottom A group of nomads crosses a pasture in the Dzakar chu valley; like farmers, they move on foot and carry their knapsacks on their backs with the strap passing in front of the shoulders. They sometimes use a horse or yak to transport awkward or heavy loads.

animal are eaten immediately while the meat is cut and dried in the cold air. Dry meat is particularly precious and constitutes the provisions for the journey when the tents are packed up and it is time to move.

Men on horseback arrive from the lane between the dilapidated walls, black silhouettes against the star-studded sky. The yaks move somnolently in the freezing air. The herdsmen place their packs on their chosen animals, arrange the load and then attach small prayer flags. As the sky begins to brighten, a woman pours everyone the last drop of hot tea and the group starts on its way, looking like a cloth that winds close-knit and silent up the slope of the mountain. The men go first on horseback and women and children come last, walking slowly to the irregular and multi-toned rhythm of the bells.

Halfway between nomads and farmers there are the semi-nomads, *samadrog*, who live in a sort of farmhouse, work in the fields but also own livestock. They mostly live in the less accessible areas of farming valleys and base their economy on grazing and farming resources combined. Their lives are organized around their house which is occupied by the family. Traditionally, semi-nomadic families have often been polyandrous even if, for different reasons, this type of family structure also existed among farmers and nomads. Although it is increasingly rare, such a family may still be found, more probably in rural areas.

Crouching in front of the hearth, the woman shakes the scorching pan in which she has poured the grains of barley to be roasted. The fire lights up her gentle, intent face. Around her are her youngest children, the most recent of the seventeen she has brought into the world. Seventeen children and five husbands, all brothers.

112 top, centre, bottom and 113 bottom In remote areas away from demographic controls, Tibetans have many children. Accustomed to contact with animals from an early age, they are sent to work in the fields when still young or to take the animals to graze. A 1995 survey in a village in Dzakar chu valley found that families have an average between 3 and 4 children that expressed the wish to go to school.

"This way our land will not be split up and our livestock will stay ours", smiles the second-born brother, the one that looks after the animals. *The eldest works in the fields, the fourth is a merchant, the other two are still young, they still have time to decide …*

"And the third?"

"Oh, he wasn't interested. He went to Lhasa. So nothing was left for him…".

It was him, the third-born rebel, who had accompanied us to his family house in the village for the losar, *the Tibetan New Year. Despite the pungent cold, the house has been cleaned and renovated and the best food prepared. The master of the house — the eldest brother — traces auspicious signs on the pillars of the house using bits of butter and a little later*

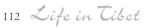

112-113 Children maintain a strong link with their mother during much of their childhood, following her around as she does her work, as shown in this picture. A mother, who in this case is probably responsible for maintenance of the road, has left her son wrapped up in a pile of blankets so that she can keep an eye on him while she works.

113 top Local communities are attempting to create schools to meet the needs of families and to prevent new generations from growing unable to read and write. Usually the building is constructed using local labour with the help of a governmental or private subsidy while teachers are paid by the government. Children are taught to read and write Tibetan and to do simple sums.

114 top, 114-115 Instead of using yak-skin for their tents, Tibetan nomads in many areas of Qinghai use the Mongol yurt. This is made from a cleverly constructed framework of wooden rods covered with mats of felted wool. Assembly and disassembly is a long and difficult business requiring time and skill.

114 bottom As in the Himalayan regions, rivers in Tibet have always created problems to movement for which ingenious solutions like yak-skin boats and suspended bridges have been devised. When the span is not too great and the crosspieces are reasonably large, the bridge does not sway much and even allows animals to cross.

115 bottom left Turquoise is one of the most popular stones among Tibetans who believe that the negative vibrations of the wearer are attracted out of the person into the stone. "Old" turquoises, i.e. those that have been worn, also have an important commercial value.

will place the new prayer flags on the roof; at dawn the mistress of the house had blessed the water that has not yet been touched by the rays of the sun of the first day of the year. With pride, the eldest brother indicates his still frozen fields that stretch to the northern limit of the village. With a proud glance, the second brother points to a well-fed herd of yak beyond a dry stone wall and, in a paddock further off, a herd of sheep around a pile of straw. In May, after the Spring festival, he will take them up the mountain to return in autumn. The third brother, the merchant, has only just returned after a long trip. He has brought with him rubber boots for the children, a pressure cooker, and coloured ribbons

for the hair of the women. Everyone has his role to play.

"And the other two?"

"For the moment they act as help, later they will play their part, as husbands too".

"But ... how do you arrange things, practically speaking?"

"Well, they just leave their shoes outside the door - so the others understand...".

The arrangement of one wife with more than one husband, generally brothers, is the most common form of polygamy in Tibet in every social class but other models are not rare either. There are women that share the same husband, or a father and son may share a common wife, provided, of course, that she is not the mother of the son. Such situations are generally managed with elegance and naturalness. Given the elaborate marriage arrangements, extra-marital relations are tolerated with casualness as

115 bottom right Nomads in the eastern regions live in such harmony with their animals that their lives are regulated by the beasts' biological rhythms. It is usually the children, who love to climb up on yak large backs, that take them to pasture.

long as they are conducted with tact and discretion. Jokingly, a Tibetan says, "the houses of my friends are filled with my children, and my house is filled with the children of my friends".

Today polygamy is prohibited. Tibetan families are officially monogamic but polyandric families, created within traditional Tibetan society and adapted to it, persist in rural areas. The authorities, however, consider it a sign of backwardness and abnormality and make strenuous efforts to abolish it.

"Polyandric and polygamic marriages are rare among farmers and herdsmen and are phenomena that violate the matrimonial laws of the state, damage the physical and mental health of those involved, and do not contribute to a full and happy family life or to a better quality of race. The party committee and the government must fully recognise the damage caused by such backward arrangements and act responsibly by indoctrinating and guiding the farmers and herdsmen towards a normal, monogamic life and towards a complete abolition of polygamic customs" (From a speech by Raidi, published in Xizang Ribao on 24 November 1998).

As they belong to an ethnic minority, the Tibetans can officially have two children, unlike the Cinese *han* who are only allowed one. This

116 As one moves eastwards, the dry, stony ground is slowly covered with more grass. The lives of the nomads here are slightly different to those of the nomads of central Tibet and they wear much gaudier ornaments.

117 top left Nomads who often have to change residence gladly use a portable loom, made from simple pieces of wood, for weaving sheep and yak wool. The long woven material is felted and used to make clothes, blankets and tent coverings.

117 bottom left Work in the fields is often the responsibility of the women who wear ornaments and elaborate hairstyles even when doing their everyday tasks. The picture shows a woman with her hair divided into numerous plaits milking a dri or female yak.

117 top right In eastern regions, the nomads generally live in camps made up of few yurts around which the men and animals roam. The small tent villages are regularly moved following fixed grazing routes which to a foreigner appear haphazard and absolutely unpredictable.

117 bottom right A woman in a yak-hair tent carries out the long and tiring business of preparing butter. The same task is performed in different places using tools that vary a great deal: possibilities are a leather bag, a modern plastic bowl or the large churn as seen in this picture.

118 top Despite the strong modern tendency towards a settled lifestyle, also favoured by the government, the tent is still the fundamental element around which nomad life is organized. It houses all generations of the family and the traditional altar with its equipment and sacred images.

118 bottom Next to the hearth, a woman is preparing one of the commonest drinks on the Tibetan plain — tea salted with butter.
In a country where sugar was unknown, tea was given energy content by dissolving a large dob of butter and mixing a handful of salt in a local churn.

119 top The nomads move around very varied types of terrain, from the grasslands of the east (in the picture) to the desert steppes of westernmost Tibet.

119 bottom Next to the large pot, the family watches as cheese is being made. As occurs in the Alps, the whey is boiled once the butter has been produced. A sort of cottage cheese is obtained from the curd which is either eaten fresh or, more often, dried.

118-119 Kindling and yak dung burn in the tent hearth and the smoke exits through the top hole in the black covers. The fire is a powerful cohesion element around which the members of the family and the neighbours gather. The domestic life of sipping tea, eating, singing and gossiping takes place next to the fire.

120 top The "furniture" of Tibetan nomad tents does not include tables or chairs so meals are taken sitting around the hearth using a bowl and spoon. Occasionally, chopsticks are used but often just hands. The knife used is the long-bladed tool used for all facets of nomad life.

120 centre In some regions, especially in the east, a stone hearth is used which makes cooking easier. Besides salted tea with butter, tsampa soup is made by cooking barley flour and throwing in a few entire grains.

120 bottom Vegetables and other greens are not widespread in Tibetan diets although much appreciated, including nettles which are called "Milarepa's food" after the famous ascetic. A legend recounts that this was practically the only food Milarepa ate while he was a hermit.

121 The portrait of this Tibetan woman shows her sipping chang, a drink that is nourishing, thirst-quenching and also used in rituals. Before drinking, Tibetan devotees dip the ring finger of their right hand in the drink and spray it up while reciting a mantra.

demographic law is fully applied in urban areas and is gradually being extended into the countryside.

The presence of farmers, *shingpa*, in Tibet since ancient times is shown by archaeological remains of which one of the oldest in Tibet was discovered in Chugong not far from Lhasa. Lines of foundations of houses or refuges in which men lived around 3000-4000 BC can be made out among the irregularly laid stones. We know that the inhabitants cultivated cereals from the remains of wheat grains found and we know that they also bred pigs and other animals that lived in pens from the traces of excrement. Tombs indicate that they buried their dead. Their tools, pottery shards and objects made from bones and small pieces of jade tell us they were creative and imaginative. Together with other finds in the areas roundabout, these discoveries define what is referred to as the Neolithic Culture in central Tibet. Mythology also tells us about ancient farming activities in which there is a frequent description of lakes that used to cover the country but which made way for forests and plains rich with animals, birds and human beings. Several versions of a widely known myth tell of the origin of the Tibetan people in which references to the transition to a farming civilization are clear.

One day Chenresi, the god of compassion, descended to earth and went to the valley of Yarlung. He disguised himself as a monkey and wandered around the countryside until he came to a grotto where he met a *dü*, a she-demon of the rocks. The two lay together and the children resulting from their union became the forefathers of the Tibetan race. The monkey made a gift of five treasures to his descendants, the five cereals – barley, wheat, rice, sesame and soya – which would allow the species to continue. And so the first field was cultivated near the current city of Tsethang where the Yarlung valley meets the valley of the Brahmaputra.

Despite the mythical images of a green and luxuriant world, agricultural Tibet is limited to the strips surrounding the rivers and their tributaries. With the exception of the extreme eastern zones

where the Brahmaputra flows through meadows and woods, the rest of its course passes through deserts and rocky areas which become green oases where tributaries join the main river. These are the sites of villages and even cities. Village houses, their courtyards filled with domestic animals, either stand at the edge of fields protected by dry stone walls or are grouped around the monastery or castle to which they belonged. Lanes between the fields and houses wind around and over the canals that are used to irrigate the fields.

The art of channelling water in Tibet is an ancient one, just as it is in all mountain areas of central-southern Asia from the Himalayas to the Karakorum to the Hindu Kush. Irrigation was mentioned in the Dunhuang documents when they chronicled the first kings of Tibet; they speak of prince Rulakye who "dug the earth and collected

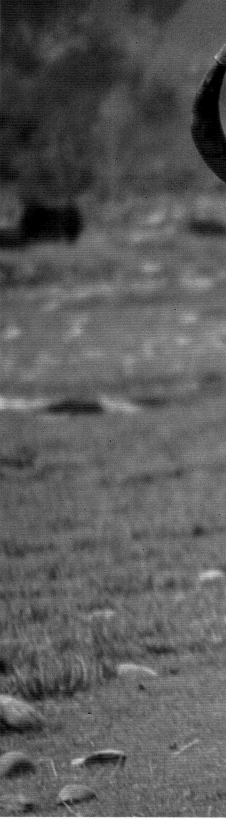

122 top Scything, gathering and piling sheaves of cereals is women's work. Barley is the most common crop at high altitude while corn grows lower down.

122 bottom After the ears have been carried away, the straw must be removed from the fields. Then the yaks and the sheep are ushered in to devour every edible fibre and fertilize the soil.

122-123 Ploughing is one of the fundamental activities in farming life and the start date is decided by divination. The stemmed plough is drawn by yaks wearing coloured ribbons and as soon as the field is completed, a pole with prayer flags attached is planted in the soil.

123 bottom left Once they have been dried, the barley grains are toasted and ground to prepare tsampa. *The traditional, heavy hand-operated grinder has now almost everywhere been replaced by water-mills.*

123 bottom right Tractors are increasingly used in farming. They are Chinese-made, small and economical and are purchased by village heads and enterprising farmers that hire their labour out to others.

water from the heights of the valley in canals". The accounts of the founding of Samye describe how Padmasambhava (presented by later tradition as a wizard who was responsible for many miracles) was above all a water expert who was able to perform the "miracle" of making fields fertile. In the 14th century, the chronicle of Shekar tells us that "with the water that ran through many channels, the Nelung plain became very fertile, the fields multiplied and the grain grew so heavy that it was necessary to strengthen the granaries. A tank was dug in each village to collect the night water. A register was created to record the water due to each farmer".

The area of the country occupied by agriculture represents about two-sevenths of the whole country. Farming takes place at an altitude that is considered low in Tibet but which is, nevertheless, between 11,000-14,000 feet above sea level. This means that the human body still has to cope with the problems suffered by the nomads though to a lesser degree. The body still has to adapt to lower oxygen levels, defend itself from ultra-violet rays and protect itself from the cold. Here the physical and psychological adaptation of the farmers is prodigious and quite the equal of the nomads. Their working techniques are primitive, though perhaps only from a western viewpoint. The tools they use are the hoe, the spade, the shovel, the very simplest type of plough pulled by a yak, the sickle, panniers and the cart; total reliance is placed on the use of hands and shoulders. Tibetan farmers pass a great deal of their time bent over the ground as they work from dawn to dusk for most of the year. They grow barley, soya, mustard, buckwheat, turnips, onions, garlic and, for the past two centuries, potatoes. Each phase of the work is accompanied by ceremonies to propitiate the gods and to beseech fertility. Prayer flags are planted in the middle of the fields during seeding and red

symbolic bows adorn yaks as they plough. In spring, many villages celebrate the *chökhor*, a procession around the fields to allow the holy books to extend their blessing to the ground.

At first light of dawn, the inhabitants of the village went up to the monastery to take the books and place them, each one, on top of the pannier. Now they are in procession behind the officiating monk. The murmur of mantra *accompanies them to the rhythm of the 108 handheld rosary beads. At mid-morning, they stop at the first of the four stations that correspond to the four cardinal points of the compass where they rest their loads. They pray with the Lama and then take out their bags of* tsampa, *the flat breads, the small tins of* chang *and the thermos with salted tea. They eat, offering each other the delicacies, then they begin to sing and start the* shabdro, *the traditional local dance. They halt obediently at the call of the Lama, take up their loads once more and start off for the next station. In the evening, happy and a little drunk, they take the holy books back to the monastery. During the night, huge rumbles of thunder announce that rain is*

124-125 This is the harvest festival in Dzongkha in central western Tibet. Different theatre groups, singers and dancers, alternate on the grass "stage" for a whole week. A stick in the centre topped by a green branch supports the red flag and the portrait of Mao.

124 bottom Inhabitants from neighbouring villages also visit the festival in the local capital. They put up white tents in a general camp where they socialize and drink many cups of chang.

125 top Dzongkha festivals have been revived over the past years. The moving force behind their rebirth was an ex-monk persecuted during the Cultural Revolution who later became mayor. There have been many figures like the mayor, especially during the 1980's, who fought to revive Tibetan traditions and culture.

125 bottom The women of Bodong celebrate a particular festival wearing the costumes and head-dresses of Tsang. The complete works of the founder of the philosophy of the local monastery have just been returned and the inhabitants of the village have erected a large tent and rehearsed traditional songs and dances for the occasion.

falling from the sky.

In July when the crops are almost ripe, the risk of hail is very real. To keep it at bay, the farmers celebrate rituals that continue until harvest time, another event also accompanied by prayers and festivals. The sheaves are gathered in the courtyards where the ears of corn wait to be separated from the grain beneath the feet of animals and people even though mechanical threshing machines now exist in the larger centres.

The peasants' houses are constructed using dried mud; they have a flat roof made from dried clay used for drying crops in the sun and a small yard in front of the door where most of the domestic activities take place. Hygienic facilities, if they exist, are monumental: they are built on two floors separated by a hole, the lower of which is regularly cleaned out.

Many villages have grown to become small towns if not actually cities. The traditional dried clay houses are flanked by the increasingly prevalent, modern, square, cement buildings covered with sheet roofing. The modern town is where the government offices, postal service, health facilities, petrol distributor and eating houses exist; this is also where merchants display their everyday indispensable items, usually of modest quality.

Trading has always been practised by everybody in Tibet even if the figure of the traditional merchant, now slowly being transformed into a modern businessman, is linked to small and large towns, yet, not infrequently, traders will be found in rural areas on the look-out for farming products, cashmere or traditional objects to sell. The traditional image of the merchant is of a robust, attentive, loyal and deeply religious man with a canny business sense. He knows how to conduct himself in all circumstances and which opportunities to take advantage of, but he is also willing to put himself at risk and go to extraordinary trouble. Above all, he is able to walk for days at a time with his animals along the old caravan routes that follow the rivers, wind through hills and over passes, and which cross towns and

cities. He stops off in small towns that generally stand at the intersection of two or more caravan routes. In the bustle of the crowd, the merchants have time to rest, swap stories, drink a little, gamble and exchange goods. They remove the loads from their animals and give them to other merchants who, with other yaks, continue along a section of the road that they know well and is therefore safer. This is the ancient system of successive links in the chain that connects the great plains in the north with the southern slopes of the Himalayas. In this system, the yak (the castrated male) is the means of transporting heavy loads. He is the "lorry" though real lorries using ex-*yakpa* (yak herders) as drivers are becoming more common as the road network expands. If the yak is the lorry, the horse is the car. Horses have always been considered the most valuable of animals in Tibet as they are the only ones capable of

126 left and 127 top Roads in Tibet have been built by the Chinese administration. Although constructed using a certain expertise, they are no match for the geologically unstable terrain. The rain provokes much damage and frequent landslips: vehicles that get bogged down or turn over are the order of the day.

126 bottom Transport difficulties in Tibet are a permanent state of affairs: with a lorry stuck in the ditch and unable to continue, the only thing to do is wait for another. Patience is indispensable for anyone wishing to travel around the Roof of the World.

126-127, 127 centre Continual road maintenance is required to repair damaged spots. To clear the carriageway and remove the earth without the help of tractors, shovels are used with an ingenious "chain action" that, sometimes accompanied by a song, achieves a suitable result and reduces the effort a mite.

providing rapid movement over large distances. Another means of transportation, less well-known but just as used, is the sheep which might be compared to a van if the metaphor is continued. It is still possible to come across load-carrying sheep on the old routes, tottering slightly under their small packsaddles of salt or wheat. In the evening, their drivers group the sheep and settle them down for the night still carrying their loads while the drivers themselves sleep under a tent.

"We move twice a year", the oldest man says after pondering the cassette-recorder with a glance, "Now we are loaded with salt. We are going to Kalimpong to exchange it. We'll come back in spring carrying rice, wheat and sugar. And also horse harnesses, prayer flags, transistor radios, Swiss watches...".

Status symbol consumer goods are one of the factors that are changing the face of the country,

even in remote areas. It is one effect of the use of the *yuan* as a means of exchange instead of bartering for goods but also a result of the new communications system. Television, radio, telephones and the new road system - despite its limitations due to geographical difficulties - are creating a network of contacts in a country that has until now always been isolated and non-communicative.

Following on the heels of the wave of battery-operated transistor radios, dish aerials now sprout up to hear the voice of Beijing or Lhasa wherever there is electricity supplied by a power station or generator. This is most likely to occur at the *shang* (town council) and the local administration takes advantage of it. Like the Chinese, the Tibetans are fascinated by television. A hotel may not have toilets but it must have a colour television in every room.

Statistics tell us that in 1997 there were 107 televisions for every 100 urban families, 96 washing machines, 68 refrigerators, 38 cameras, 68 scooters and 188 bicycles (*Xinhua*, 27 January 1999). Telephones used to be a military monopoly until a few years ago but are beginning to spread. County towns are beginning to offer a public service, mobile phones are permitted and even the use of satellite telephones is allowed. Nevertheless, it is the spread of roads that is bringing most change.

Once, merchants' caravans used to follow routes that were little more than paths or sheep-tracks. When they reached a river or stream, the travellers crossed at fords or found a yak-hide boat that would carry them to the other side in return for a little salt, butter or piece of cloth. Heavier loads had to wait for winter when ice made the crossing more solid. Large bridges over the Brahmaputra were first built

in the 15th century by Tangtong Gyalpo, a religious master and skilful "civil engineer". They were built of iron chains fixed to huge stone pillars on each side of the river and some are still in use.

With her chupa held tight around her legs, the full pannier on her back, the woman climbs up onto the pillar of stones that supports the bridge. She murmurs a mantra as she hangs a prayer flag, she looks around, rests her hands on the shiny rings on each side and begins to walk. Her feet advance securely avoiding the poorly attached wooden crosspieces. In the centre of the river, she is forced to jump over a little hole; her load wavers and the woman slows as the bridge sways dreadfully over the rapids. After about ten minutes, she comes to a halt with a jump onto the other bank where a lorry is waiting. When the body of the lorry has been filled with people, it will set off for the village up a rough path. Old and rusty, the lorry got left on the other side when the new road bridge collapsed one night when the river was in flood.

130-131 *The traditional figure of the merchant is tending to disappear. In general he has become a businessman but he can still be met with his caravan of yaks as he accompanies mountain climbers or tourists towards the high mountains when his load is made up of tents, equipment and food. Here we see a column in the Karma chu valley as it approaches the east wall of Mount Everest.*

It was the Chinese authorities that brought roads to Tibet during a spate of innovations that has profoundly altered Tibetan society. When the communes were dissolved during the 1980's on the orders of Deng and Hu Yaobang, the administration was reorganized on the Chinese model. In Tibet certain traditional elements re-emerged. Local people able to read and write, i.e. those few that had been able to study, were selected to be its staff, especially in the remote areas where life was particularly hard. Responsible for a local community, some of these people took on a role that, in certain aspects, resembled that of the old village-heads. In remote areas it was not uncommon to come across moving combinations of the modern and the traditional, the results of the cultural liberalization of the 1980's, but unfortunately those combinations are now rapidly disappearing.

The final bluish wisps of incense smoke rise from the roofs of the houses. The sun has risen and a new day has begun. At 8 o'clock, the old loudspeaker on the corner of the shang begins to crackle. It is connected to the radio to broadcast music and the day's news. A red flag flutters at the top of a

pole near the dish aerial. In his room the shangtang *(mayor) is getting ready. He wears his blue-grey ceremonial suit with the high collar, patent leather shoes and he ties his dark red* chupa *over the top. He places the necessary objects in the front flap, then mounts his horse that awaits him with his best saddle and sets off followed by the procession of people. All the people of the village will participate with him in the ancient ceremony of blessing the fields.*

The structure of the administration of the Autonomous Region of Tibet reflects that of the People's Republic of China; in other words, most of the power is held by the Party under the guidance of the party secretary. In addition to this there is the government under the direction of a President (a Tibetan, according to the constitution) and other bodies that generally have only a nominal importance. This structure is the same in the seven prefectures which make up the Autonomous Region of Tibet and also in the counties where it is gradually simplified. In the town councils (*shang*) only the mayor (*shangtang*) and the party secretary with their respective assistants are left. Below them there are the village-heads. Each unit has precise responsibilities — for example, the health and education facilities and also responsibility for the recovery and care of cultural relics — but these are slowly being limited and made more local. Despite thousands of difficulties, the local cadres occasionally manage to make the voice of the population heard so that living conditions might be improved, for instance, with the construction of a school.

After travelling for hours on the desert plateau, a school can be made out at the base of the hill where the village stands. A low, wide building with a door decorated in bright colours opens onto an internal courtyard. It is one of the innumerable village schools built with great good will by the local community, despite having little money or other means, for which the shangtang *has managed to get teachers assigned by the county government although the school severely lacks educational tools. Knots of children play with an old ball. In a classroom, the board shows numbers and Tibetan words. A lady teacher wearing the traditional* chupa *and turquoise and coral jewellery around her neck offers the traditional salted tea. "Solgia she — Drink, guest, please try our traditional drink".*

132-133 The combination of snow and ice can create exceedingly lovely but equally cold landscapes. In the photograph a rider tranquilly proceeds on his way through the snowy woods of Kham; only Tibetans, who are physically accustomed to and suitably protected against the low temperatures, are able to withstand the winter cold at high altitude.

132 bottom Yaks try to tear the sparse blades of grass that push above the frozen crust on the snowy steppe. They are frequently looked after by a woman. Although tasks are roughly divided, women generally have more to do.

133 top In winter, nomads try to camp close to rivers or streams that have not completely frozen over so they can supply their needs without too much difficulty. If all is frozen, the only thing to do is melt the snow or ice but doing so uses up precious fuel.

133 bottom Putting up and taking down camp is not an easy job, especially when everything has been frozen by a recent snowfall. On the hearth in the centre — kept on from first thing in the morning to last thing at night — a pot of warming tea is boiling.

134-135 When on the move, traditional merchants wrap themselves in skins and travel on horseback. This was the most common method of transport before roads and vehicles began to appear and before yak-drivers turned into lorry drivers.

136-137 As one looks east from the roof of the Potala, Lhasa stretches out of view down its lovely valley. The name of the city reflects the magnificence of the place: in Tibetan, "Lha" are the gods and "sa" is the place. Today there are modern buildings everywhere, even filling the countryside that used to stretch between the Dalai Lama's old palace and the Jokhang.

136 bottom Golden yaks are one of the most suitable symbols of Lhasa today. They stand in the centre of a roundabout that regulates the traffic at an important junction. A group of monks in the foreground is undisturbed by the passing of the cars.

" **• • •** at a bend, a hill-like heap of stones marks the spot where the adoring pilgrims can get the first glimpse of the Potala's gilded spires. Each pilgrim is supposed to say a prayer at the moment and to throw a stone to raise the the heap. ... Towards noon we reached the Potala. Rather than a palace, it is a hill in itself, an outgrowth of the rock underlying it, as irregular and whimsical as nature's work ... Our caravan filed off past the Potala, reeled to and fro and broke its ranks ... it turned towards the river and stopped in the Ghiavolinca, a shady park of willows and poplars. ... The town of Lhasa speads east of the Potala palace ...". These were the first impressions made on the scholar Giuseppe Tucci in 1949 by Lhasa, the city of the gods. Tucci was one of the first westerners to enter the sacred city with the eye of a scholar. His writings are filled with technical observations on customs and religion and his travel stories are written in the language of a pilgrim fascinated by the world he is witnessing and for which he is filled with admiration and warmth.

Even half a century later, the traveller who goes to Lhasa will be won over by the crisp, thin air, by the friendly people and by the remains of a great past but it is no longer the roofs of the Potala that arouse the first wonder and eagerness. The eyes of

137 top Glass and cement are the preferred materials for the latest generation of buildings erected in the style of large Chinese cities. The huge Chinese and Tibetan Bookstore and the phantasmagorical Bank of China are perfect examples.

137 centre Potala Square is the brand new architectural feature of the city. Motor vehicles are able to pass through the square on a road flanked by two wide cycle paths.

137 bottom The large Jokhang Square is one of the places where the traditional atmosphere of Lhasa can still be found, particularly in the morning. What remains of the old Tibetan district is found behind and to the sides of the square where, for the moment, life continues unhurriedly to the rhythm of the past.

the visitor who arrives from afar first alight upon a multitude of modern buildings; the entrance to the city no longer passes below the Potala, instead a wide band of asphalt with two cycle lanes runs parallel to the river Kyichu. You pass innumerable military huts that make Lhasa "the safest city in the world" and you glimpse a long row of small, "elegant", modern pagodas, small shops, tea houses and the brothels of the modern Lhasa. Potala Square lies below the palace like a huge stage paved with grey stone slabs and illuminated by bunches of neon lights. It connects the majestic steps of the Palace with the sweet little lake in the "park shaded by willows and poplars". A perfect expanse, the square of heaven, the Tian'anmen of Tibet.

Like other ancient cities, the different epochs and different styles that mark Lhasa tell the story of its people in its stones. Under the ancient name of Rasa, "place of the goats" or "fenced place", this locality was selected by the Tibetan kings to be the capital of the kingdom. Consequently, it was transformed into Lhasa, the "place of the gods". The Jokhang was built here, Tibet's central cathedral. The devotional and mercantile circuit that surrounds it, the Barkhor, spreads out down narrow lanes between stone houses, tapered walls and blue bordered door-curtains grey from the dust. Here men and women with their *chupa*, prayer wheel and rosary in hand live their lives to the rhythm of prayers. At dawn they visit the Jokhang, burn incense, light the butter lamps and prostrate themselves before the portal; in the evening they

138-139 Having passed through the large central gate, the visitor enters the courtyard of Jokhang temple, a holy, open-air space surrounded by a colonnade. Undisturbed, the Dalai Lama used to watch the functions in the courtyard from his apartment at the top left.

138 bottom The decorations on the top of the golden roofs are filled with symbols and religious meanings. As with painted images, the function of dragons and the terrifying images of gods is to defend the religion and keep evil spirits away.

139 top Seen from the terrace on the first floor, the magnificent central section of the Jokhang is crowned with golden roofs and spires. The temple contains the holiest and most worshipped site of Tibetan Buddhism, the chapel of the Jobo.

139 centre The holy space of the large courtyard is beautifully created by the double row of tapered wooden columns painted with red lacquer.

139 bottom The details of the roof over the Dalai Lama's apartment reveal the imagination of its architect and the skill of its builders. The fixed motif often found elsewhere in the complex follows the alternation of dragons, mythological birds and symbolic spires to create an effect of brilliance that is deeply loved by Tibetans.

Ancient and modern Lhasa

140 *A great demonstration of veneration a Tibetan is capable of is the* chak, *the prostration of the entire body while reciting a particular holy formula. To perform the 108* chak *prescribed by the rosary, devotees often protect their hands, feet and knees.*

141 *top and 141 centre Devotees still stop on the old and worn paving in front of the Jokhang gateway in the morning, then find some space and joyously begin their worship. It is a ceremony that lasts for hours, accompanied by the murmuring of prayers and whorls of incense smoke.*

141 *bottom The grandness of the Jokhang square becomes apparent when seen from the roof of the temple. Inside the stone enclosure in the centre grows the willow tree that tradition says dates from the time of the Tibetan kings. The enclosure to the right protects the stele that records the reciprocal non-aggression pact made between the Tibetans and Chinese in 821-822 AD.*

circle the Barkhor reciting *mantra* and turning the prayer wheel. Each day pilgrims from all over Tibet crowd in front of the Jokhang, sometimes having travelled long distances. They arrive on foot, on horseback and by boat but today they mostly arrive by lorry. They have been squeezed together in the back of the lorry for days with their scarves wrapped around their faces to protect them from the cold and dust, thrown about by the bumps in the road, hands tightly gripping the bag that holds their tea thermos and dry meat. At Lhasa they fix themselves up as best they can in the houses of friends, acquaintances or fellow-villagers and begin their devotions.

At first light the braziers that surround the Jokhang begin to burn once more. A string of pilgrims awaits, their hands filled with incense, powder, leaves and branches collected in the mountains and brought to the square to be burned. The first devotee kneels and throws in his handful. The fire flares up, a whitish cloud of smoke billows through the air and reaches the Dharma wheel and the deers that crown the pediment of the golden roofs. *Om mani padme hum. In front of the great door, beyond the stele that records the historical pact of non-aggression with the Chinese, laymen and monks, men and women and sometimes even children, perform the ritual genuflections, the* chak. *The young nun with reddened cheeks and a lively manner, her habit held tight with two large clamps, raises her joined hands above her head, her lips, her heart — the mind, the speech and the body — then kneels and touches her head to the soil while her hands rest on the ground*

alongside her hips. Then she pushes her hands forwards and stretches the length of her body, her arms out in front of her head. She rises and begins again: one, two, three, one hundred and eight times, one for each bead on the rosary beside her hands on the ground that enables her to keep count. One thousand times one hundred – the eight do not count – are necessary to achieve the first initiation, the first step towards enlightenment.

Some worshippers follow the concentric devotional paths around the Jokhang while performing *chak*. The shortest circuit is around the inside of the temple while the Barkhor, the "intermediate circuit", follows its walls and is completed in a clockwise direction. The Barkhor is also the traditional commercial centre of Lhasa and a little bit of everything can be found on its stalls: clothes, large padded jackets, locally produced fur hats, artificial silk, *thanka*, religious articles, Nepalese handicrafts, traditional jewellery copied with uncertain skill, finely carved yak bone pendants, turquoise and other stones though often imitation, then thermos flasks, bowls, pots and pans, linen, shoes, torches and yellow packets of *ghee*, the Nepalese margarine that almost everywhere has replaced the traditional yak butter used for devotional purposes.

The outermost ritual route is the Lingkhor. This passes through modern districts of the city but many devotees follow it. It may happen that on a crowded arterial road, the traffic may have to be stopped because an old woman has suddenly

142 top right and centre One of the most common rituals in Lhasa is the khora, i.e. the journey that devotees make around the walls of the Jokhang whilst praying. This is the famous route of the Barkhor, filled with ritual significance and also a picturesque market. Stalls sell prayer flags and holy objects but also all types of consumer goods.

142 top left, 142 bottom and 143 Hundreds of people from all social classes complete the khora of the Barkhor every day. Most common are the elderly and the monks with prayer wheel in hand but there are also the young, women and even children who perplexedly follow their mothers as they perform their devotions.

appeared out of a side street performing *chak*, unworried that her *khora* is crossed by an asphalt road. The drivers stop, sometimes smiling, sometimes cursing, but always patient.

The roads in Lhasa's modern town planning have been designed with a set-square. In place of the marshy, stony areas that separated the district around the Jokhang from that around the base of the Potala where Songtsen Gampo's goats used to graze, now there are large avenues, cycle routes, advertising hoardings and flowerbeds decorated with large monuments that divide the traffic lanes at junctions. To either side there are small and large shops, discotheques, offices, small restaurants, buildings in "tile style" or "blue glass style" which remind one of the crowded Chinese cities. But there are also traditional walls made from large stones and wooden framed windows to comply with the "modern Tibetan style" recently

144-145 *In the court of the Jokhang, rows and rows of butter lamps burn continuously below the porch in front of the gate that opens into the temple. A very common ritual gesture is to light 108 of them but in order to do so, there might be a long waiting list.*

144 bottom *On special occasions, the holy open-air space in the courtyard of the Jokhang is turned into a theatre for large religious ceremonies. As the resident monks are only responsible for maintenance, it is necessary to invite monks from other monasteries, especially Sera and Drepung, in order to celebrate the rituals suitably in the presence of a high-ranking lama.*

145 top Maitreya, the Buddha of the Future, is shown in one of the three recently made statues that dominate the central room of the Jokhang. The statue of Chenresi, the bodhisattva *of compassion also known by the Sanskrit name Avalokiteshvara, stands in the centre and Guru Rinpoche, or the famous Padmasambhava, is on the left.*

145 bottom In the central chapel of the Jokhang sits the Jobo, the most famous, most venerated and best loved statue of Buddha in Tibet. It is said to have been brought to Tibet by Songtsen Gampo's Chinese wife and, following a period of uncertainty, to have found its permanent resting place in the Jokhang.

Tibetans from the urban middle class made up of party and government cadres, intellectuals and businessmen that pragmatically and successfully collaborate with the financial and academic worlds of China and other countries. While the guest sips the jasmin tea offered with traditional sweets mixed with lollies, one of the Tibetans talks on a mobile phone. In the next door room he can hear a fax and through the half-closed door he glimpses the screen of a computer connected to Internet.

Even Tibet can access now and which foreigners can use in places like the famous Barkhor Café. A press release from the Xinhua agency on 4 February 1999 stated that "last year the central government of China spent 600 million yuan laying a fibre optic cable to connect Tibet to the north-west provinces. ... In the last six months, the Telecom office in Lhasa has registered 300 Internet users. ... The authorities have plans for public cyber cafés to be opened to meet the user demand".

Besides its leap into the information age, Lhasa has renovated its basic infrastructures and even built a sewage and fresh water system. Situated on the course of the river Kyichu in an area of abundant underground water reserves, Lhasa has never had problems of this kind. The wells gave ample water while the hygiene facilities were cleaned regularly and exploited to fertilize the fields. Now that the population has increased more than five-fold since 1950 and that the "product" is no longer used in agriculture, on the lower parts of the walls of the old houses the overfilled latrines ooze unpleasant brownish stains.

It is not easy to restore what remains from the past — the buildings are often dilapidated, the fixtures are rotten, the roofs are no longer watertight and the walls look dirty and crumbling — so the public administration opted for demolition to create space for new districts built in "gaudy Chinese" and "modern

introduced into the city's regulation plans. They are all styles by which "the simultaneous existence of the several "Lhasas" that today crowd on top of one another to create space and supremacy in the evolving city can be recognized", according to Robert Barnett, writer and specialist in matters related to modern Tibet. Here and there, flimsy "socialist-style" buildings can be seen that house institutions dedicated to study, preservation of the cultural heritage and promotion of commercial initiatives.

Four flights of steps and a freezing corridor, marked at intervals by "night pots" filled with sand for putting out cigarette butts, brought the visitor towards the office. The wooden door opened onto a vast and slightly smoky room and he was asked to sit down on a brown, fake leather sofa. In front of him on the other side of the room sit the partners that have invited him to discuss the project. They are

146 top The Potala is Lhasa's best-known building and the symbol of Tibet. It was called the "palace of a thousand rooms" by the Tibetans when "thousand" signified a large number beyond human calculation.

146 centre The white palace stands large over the internal court. The flight of steps that leads to the upper floors begins just inside the large gateway. The steps are divided into three sections, one for going up, one for coming down and one for the exclusive use of the Dalai Lama.

146 bottom The most impressive entrance to the Potala is on the south side. Protected by a heavy curtain, it opens onto a superb flight of steps that connects the seat of the God-Ruler to the world of mortals.

Tibetan" styles. Where the old houses have not been destroyed and loving and skilled renovation has been applied, the price paid for anonymous modernization becomes clear. Important monuments that have been restored with care and abundant resources have created a perfect "museum style"; one such example is the Potala palace.

On visiting days, the Potala is filled with an uninterrupted procession guided around the "thousand rooms" of the ancient palace. Yellowish light from a lantern fitfully illuminates statues in a dark corridor. Statues of Tibetan kings, religious masters and holy men that diffused and carried the Buddhist religion to glory appear in the semi-darkness. Before them a small crowd listens. The smiling but slightly worried Tibetan guide describes the histories of the figures in his fragmentary English. The group leader translates piecemeal. The tourists are in late middle age with cameras slung around their necks. They listen attentively, look around and comment quietly. Then they move en masse towards the new chapel which the group ahead of them is vacating just as the first-comers of the group behind arrive. Faces drawn by the altitude and the exertion, they collect a little later in the bar where they try to recuperate some strength from a canned drink while swapping comments. At last, they arrive triumphant on the roof where they indulge in an orgy of picture taking against the backgrounds of the gilded roofs, dragons, golden symbols, balustrades overlooking Lhasa, the haze of smog over the cement factory, the white blurs of the monastic cities, the military barracks, the cement banks of the Kyichu, the phantasmagorical offices of the Bank of China and, bathed in incense smoke, Jokhang square.

People from all over the world, of all colours, speaking every language, pass through the Potala. It is a new pilgrimage in addition to, and partly in place of, the devotional journey made by pilgrims to the place where once ministers and employees of the Tibetan government zealously examined documents, received petitions, formulated edicts and celebrated propitiatory rituals — when the Potala was still the

seat of the Dalai Lama.

The Potala was built by the fifth Dalai Lama to make Lhasa the opulent and pulsating heart of Tibet. The chosen site was the Marpo ri, the red hill in front of the Jokhang, where Songtsen Gampo was supposed to have built his palace. Construction began in 1645, first with the white palace, then with the imaginative and irregularly-shaped red palace, and continued for some years until the latter was harmoniously joined to the former and to the rocks of the mountain to create the unique and spectacular complex that we see today. The death of the fifth Dalai Lama occurred before construction was complete and consequently the news was not made public. When the official announcement of his death was made, his reincarnation was already a young man who had received a secular education and who had the most varied interests. He accepted the title of the sixth Dalai Lama but refused to take

146-147 At one time the Tibetan district of Schöl stood at the feet of the Potala with a double row of small shops but today it has been turned into a massive wall in "modern Tibetan style", a lawn and a huge paved area. This is Potala Square but despite the changes, the Tibetan soul still considers that the Potala maintains its ancient significance.

147 bottom The red palace built above the white one is topped by a wide band of innumerable faggots of thin, pressed wood painted dark red. On the right in the foreground stands a mythical snow lion.

148-149, 148 bottom The section of golden roofs that crown the Potala is evidence of the genius that designed this complex. The windows of the corridors that open onto the roofs of the large rooms are protected by heavy curtains embroidered with Pelbe, the infinite knot which is repeated endlessly. It is the sign of eternity and the infinite interlacing of human history, love and harmony.

149 top This photograph shows one of the many doors in the Potala. They are frequently presented as laced and gilded metalwork structured in such a fashion that they are both solid and elegant. Dragons and other mythical animals are some of the motifs used in the decorations.

the vows. A lover of the arts, beautiful women and fun, his life was more dedicated to pleasure and secular interests than to the duties of government. A small lake had formed below the Potala when material for its construction had been dug out of the ground and in this lake, a Lu, a water spirit in the form of a dragon, had established itself. To propitiate the Lu, the sixth Dalai Lama had a small temple called the Lukhang built and dedicated to it. In this splendid and peaceful place, he used to meditate but that was not all. On the bases of his writings, we can imagine him as he passes over the small bridge at night, his figure hidden by the fronds of the willow trees on his way to a tryst in the temple. There, waiting for him there were songs accompanied by a *tamnyen* (a type of guitar) and a simple but accurate meal with his lover. Similarly, we can also picture the god-ruler as he sat in front of the magnificent frescoes, his gaze lost in thought, as he composed his songs of love, one of the masterpieces of Tibetan literature.

The Potala was the official seat of the Dalai Lama from the moment it was completed until 1959. It represented the heart of the government, the parliament, the administration and the staff school as well as containing chapels, apartments, prayer cells and tombs. The store-rooms contained indescribable treasures such as the golden insignia of

149 bottom left The large entrance to the white palace is made of red lacquered wood with heavy studs and decorations. It is topped by a row of white snow lions and the name "Gateway of Perfect Convergence" in Sanskrit and Tibetan characters.

149 bottom right The strong and proud lion of the snows is one of the recurring symbols in the sacred decorations. He may be represented alone or in a long series.

150 top left *Protective deities are also shown in the frescoes. Here we see the king of the Naga who also represents the king of the direction West in the four cardinal points of the compass.*

150 top right *There are many libraries inside the Potala. Shelving that fills entire walls is divided into compartments, each of which accommodates one book. Each holy book is replaced, wrapped in a cloth and protected by two wooden covers which might be painted, illuminated or engraved.*

the Tibetan kings, ancient weapons and manuscripts of rolled palm leaves illuminated with gold dust. The cellars contained reserves for the country and monasteries while the prison on the eastern side held important prisoners. From the end of the 18th century, the Potala remained the winter house of the Dalai Lama but every spring he was carried in a litter in a splendid procession down the avenue to the Norbulingka, the "garden of the jewel". In his autobiography, the fourteenth Dalai Lama described the joy he felt on leaving the sumptuous but gelid winter palace. For him the Norbulingka represented a celebration with its gardens, trees, fish-filled lakes and animals that he fed himself. Taking advantage of the few occasions offered to him, here he learnt the rudiments of physics, English and geography; he mastered the use of a film projector and learnt how to drive a car. The car had been a gift that was disassembled, carried over the Himalayas and reassembled in Lhasa. It was here that he met Heinrich Harrer who helped him perfect his self-taught

150 bottom *The statue seated on the throne is of the 13th Dalai Lama. An individual who had great character, he led his country wisely though with some difficulty during a period of great political and social changes.*

150-151 *The "Room of Eternal Life" on the top floor of the palace was reserved for the Dalai Lama to study the holy doctrines. The most internal room was the bedroom, furnished in monastic style with walls finely decorated like* thangka.

151 bottom Even the internal doors are magnificent. They are always lacquered and have large metal strips and elaborate studs. A long row of white lacquered snow lions stands above the gable.

knowledge. And it was from here that he fled by night in 1959, dressed as a simple Tibetan, as the mortars fired on the rebellious people.

A small temple called the Palalubuk stands in front of the Potala where Songtsen Gampo used to meditate. Inside the building, there is a deep natural cave with walls adorned with holy images and votive lamps. A monk silently prays in front of the cave: *om ah hum*. This is a magical place where for a few moments the mind is able to feel the flow of history and the slow, majestic passing of time towards infinity.

The Jokhang is the heart of Tibetan Buddhism, of Lhasa and of Tibet; it was built by Songtsen Gampo, not for personal meditation but for the glory of the Buddhist religion. Every day it is filled with crowds of pilgrims and tourists who enter to crown the holiest of pilgrimages. They enter, spinning the large prayer wheel that fills the secondary passage used as an entrance, then they disperse into the large courtyard and through a dark corridor to reach the interior. Past the row of cushions used by the monks there stand enormous statues of Maitreya (the Buddha of the future), Chenresi (the *bodhisattva* of compassion) and the great Padmasambhava. All around, chapels stand open.

Women clutching packets of *ghee*, men with the *katak* and their offering at the ready, and impatient children who thread their way through the legs of the adults all wait in the orderly file. They move forwards close to the wall and enter the various chapels a few at a time. When they emerge, stooping under the low doorways, they retake their places smiling and happy in the queue. When they arrive in front of the central chapel, they stop at the strict but benevolent sign of the supervising monk. Someone peels off to perform a hurried *chak* and scurries back into line with a small smile of complicity. The protective grate is opened and the

152-153 *This photograph shows the room where the Dalai Lama used to receive his guests. The room and its valuable paintings and rugs have all been restored to their former splendour but, though once a holy place and in continuous use, today it resembles a room in a museum.*

152 bottom *Many rooms in the Potala open onto long corridors painted with red lacquer and lit by a series of windows decorated with wooden columns. The light is filtered by heavy external curtains which partially cover the windows.*

153 top Maitreya is the bodhisattva who will become the Buddha of the future. This popular and loved divinity, seen here with his face covered in gold, is often represented with his hands at the height of his heart in the sign of teaching.

153 bottom Mythological figures and Buddhist symbols have also been etched on the small metal studs, for example, another snow lion can be seen on the right. When sacred texts mention the production and preparation of iron and wood for the construction of statues, they often also refer to Nepalese craftsmen who were especially invited to do the work. It was said that besides being of divine origin, these artisans would magically disappear, one after the other, once the work was complete.

pilgrim is bathed in light. He moves forward, happy but bewildered, to perform the *khora* further inside. In the centre of a radiance of gold, lights, white *katak* and offerings, sits Jobo, the holiest, most worshipped and most loved Buddha, the very heart of the heart.

The statue of Jobo was brought to Tibet by Songtsen Gampo's Chinese wife, princess Wencheng. It was first placed at Ramoche, the first temple built in Lhasa, and then in the Jokhang where it has remained. The Jokhang had been built by Songtsen Gampo's Nepalese wife, princess Bhirikuti, to house a statue that she had brought with her. A long time was spent searching for a suitable site for the new temple until princess Wencheng, using complex geomantic calculations, identified a demoness hidden in the soil under all of Tibet whose heart corresponded to the location of a small lake in Lhasa. This signified the spot where the temple had to be built. The first thing to be done was to sap the vital fluids from the demoness, in other words, to drain the lake and then "nail down" the demoness. A *mandala* of concentric rings and squares was created with "nails" at strategic points: these were represented by monasteries, four for the shoulders and the ankles, four for the elbows and the knees, two for the hands and two for the distant feet which were built at Buthan in the extreme west. The Jokhang was built in the centre of the *mandala*. The lake was

154 top The palaces of the Norbulingka — the name means "garden of the jewel" — are surrounded by a park to the west of the city. Their visitors include many Tibetans.

154 centre Furnished with valuable rugs, murals, thangka and furniture, the Norbulingka became the Dalai Lama's summer residence at the end of the 18th century.

154 bottom The throne of the 14th Dalai Lama in the palace of Norbulingka is empty but the white katak placed there show that his spiritual presence is permanent to Tibetans.

154-155 The summer residence of the 14th Dalai Lama was completed in 1956 from where he fled to India three years later. Currently, visitors are permitted to see his apartment with its study, work rooms and bedroom.

155 bottom The Lukhang is a temple built on a small island in the centre of a lake behind the Potala. It is connected to the banks by a small bridge and dedicated to the king of the Naga — the spirits of the waters — called "Lu" in Tibetan. The temple was built and dedicated by the 6th Dalai Lama who also used it as his personal retreat. Today the Lukhang is a small oasis of peace in a city growing increasingly frenetic.

156 top Tibetans regard rainbows as signs of particularly good omen. The very maximum that Tibetans can hope for is for one to appear over the Potala.

156 bottom left The **garuda** is a large mythological bird, half-man and half-bird of prey, that became a vehicle for Buddha. It is a common symbol in Tibet.

156 bottom right The metal in gold decorations is often embossed. Sanskrit characters often alternate with symbols to indicate all the **mantra** of the Kalachakra, the wheel of time.

drained but its echo can still be heard if you listen carefully, and with faith, with your ear to a hollow column inside the temple.

Although the Jokhang has been done up on several occasions over the centuries, the most extensive work being undertaken by the fifth Dalai Lama, the temple's structure has not been altered much. A potent symbol to be loved or desecrated, it was the beacon that illuminated the path of the faithful throughout the centuries of darkness just as it did during Buddhism's golden age.

"When the uncle-cum-minister Masham persecuted the doctrine, the temple of Rasa was transformed into a slaughterhouse, sheep carcasses were hung from the hands of all statues and entrails were wrapped around their necks."

So says the chronicle of the construction of Samye monastery referring to the youth of king Trisong Detsen when the anti-Buddhism faction took advantage for a certain time. With the Cultural Revolution over a thousand years later, the temple at Lhasa became a symbol for the

profanation of everything that represented Tibet's ancient society and culture. The Jokhang was turned into a pigsty and a storehouse, it was plundered and fired upon, and it became the theatre of chases and killings. During the 1980s, a massive work of restoration was undertaken and the temple once more became a centre of worship. Today the Jokhang is still the place loved best by Tibetans who find there some of the original paintings and statues and others that have been recreated. What has not changed is the holy and mystical atmosphere created by their presence. Yet the Jokhang continues to be a symbol-place also in a political sense, theatre of resistance and repression.

156-157 *The corners of the pagoda-type roofs of the Potala and the Jokhang are decorated with large overhanging gilded metal dragons. Not only ornamental, they are also supposed to frighten away evil spirits.*

157 bottom *Decorations on embossed metal include flowers, ritual objects, deities and, above all, the smiling Buddha seated still on a lotus flower.*

The monastic

community

158 top Monastic life continues in Tibet despite the many difficulties but on a much reduced scale compared to former times; monasteries are still an important point of cultural reference to Tibetans, especially in remote areas. The photograph shows prayer wheels in Labrang monastery.

158 centre As at Labrang, a room is dedicated to a large prayer wheel in every monastery. The prayer wheel is a huge, colourfully painted cylinder with prayers written on it in Sanskrit that revolves around a central axle. The devotee spins it clockwise and a bell rings at each completed turn.

158 bottom Monks are often asked to make prophecies. They have many tools to help them among which the most common is the tsi, a diagram used for making astrological calculations. Astrology in Tibet is a highly developed subject combining aspects of Indian, Chinese and local origin.

In his speech at the Deer Park of Sarnath, known as the First Turn of the Dharma Wheel, Buddha expressed the principles of the four noble truths: suffering, the origin of suffering, the extinction of suffering and the path that leads to the extinction of suffering. Underlying suffering is the attachment to an illusory conception of the self and worldly phenomena. Only those who achieve understanding of the impermanent nature of things and detachment from them will be able to free themselves from the cycle of reincarnations, samsara, and to attain spiritual liberation, nirvana. Renunciation is considered fundamental for progress to be made along this arduous path and monastic life is considered the best means to achieve it. The monastic community forms the third of the Three Jewels of Buddhism - Buddha (the Master himself),

Dharma (the Doctrine) and Sangha (the Community) - the three jewels in which whoever wishes to embrace Buddhism retreats. On these bases, Tibetan monasteries in the past multiplied in size at an extraordinary rate, filled with ranks of monks and nuns who dedicated themselves to the life of the spirit. Today their number has drastically fallen in Tibet; however, it is possible to witness moments of religious and everyday life in restored monasteries that recall the days of greatness described in historical documents.

October 1995. It is time for the afternoon break. The monks grouped in front of the altar are about to finish their prayers which will be followed by afternoon tea. There is much to-ing and fro-ing in the kitchen. Two sturdy monks approach the steaming pot in which the salted butter drink is boiling, they grab hold of it at the sides and begin to pour the tea into the prepared thermos flasks. As they are filled, the

158-159 Monasteries still attract a good number of adepts but, as there are limits on their numbers, only some of those who apply can be accepted. In the monastery, the youngsters learn to read the holy texts and to write while the more important monasteries offer the monks the possibility of studying a difficult and complex scholastic curriculum. The picture shows two novices having a break in the monastery of Ganden.

159 bottom One of the several roles the boys have to perform is that of a guard. Here a novice in Sakya monastery is opening a door that leads to the room dedicated to the terrifying deities.

novices pick them up and take them to the prayer room. The tea left in the pot is poured into the bowls of the poor that have gathered outside the door who in turn are surrounded by groups of whining and starving dogs. Even if the monks are few in number and their activities limited, the monastery is still functioning. But in the intense light of the sunset, the mind instinctively tends to multiply the numbers of dark red blurs of the monks' habits as they pass through the paths and up and down flights of steps; one pictures the walls as they were when new, and imagines the vitality of the original community with monks meditating, groups debating philosophy and others occupied in printing holy books.

The traditional organization of the monastery was a sort of closed community in which everyone participated. Each individual, from the abbot down to those who carried out the humblest tasks, had a part to play that contributed to the functioning of the large machine. It was a point of honour for Tibetan families to have at least one son or daughter dedicated to the Doctrine, although the monastery also frequently guaranteed a bowl of *tsampa* per day, and this brought a flux of young people of simple, intense faith to the monastery despite hardly knowing how to read. The result was that the children of poorer families often ended up as "attendants" to those that had been able to study. Peasant families living in the huts that belonged to the monastery acted as servants and were almost considered as "property". They were obliged to hand over a good part of their crops to the monastery and to perform the hard physical

work but in exchange they received material and spiritual security, religious services at death, a shelter if the need arose, and medical help from the monastery herbalist in cases of sickness.

One monk in the most important monasteries would be a doctor who had been trained by a master to identify herbs and make potions, to feel the pulse, to analyse urine and the humours, and, above all, to study the *thangka* and the holy texts handed down from the Buddha of Medicine that were fundamental to curing sicknesses of the body and mind when combined with practical skill.

Monasteries were not only dependent on the income from their properties but also on donations. The figure of the donor, the *gindak*, was officially included in the monastic liturgy with a special ritual, the *kugye*, which is still widespread today.

After finishing their chanting in the prayer room, the monks close the last page of the book and await the gindak. *The donor is a merchant who has just returned from a successful business trip and has now come to the monastery: the monks will pray for him and the blessing of the gods will continue to fall on his family and his work. The tall, strong young man, his hair plaited with a red and blue string around his head, wears a black* chupa *with blue flaps and holds a* katak *containing a roll of small denomination bank notes in his hand. At a nod from the master of ceremonies, the merchant approaches the leader of the choir and offers him a wad of notes. He repeats the gesture to the second singer and so on to each of the others, reducing the sum in correspondence with their importance. At the end of the procedure, the master accompanies the merchant to meet other monks from the cellars, the print room, the vegetable*

160 Some monasteries were successful in saving their ancient thangkha *from destruction and the greed of the merchants. The picture shows a* mandala *with Guhyasamaia in the centre, one of the supreme Tantric yogi, engaged in mystical intercourse with his consort. This 15th-century* thangkha *is held in the monastery of Sakya.*

161 top *Painting on* thangkha *is a traditional activity for monks. The cloth is cotton pulled taut at the edges and the brush has an extremely soft tip made from just a few hairs that enables precise control. In accordance with tradition, the colours are made from herbs and ground stones. A single* thangkha *may require months of work.*

161 centre *The picture on this* thangkha *is of Padmasambhava on his heavenly throne. Also known as Guru Rinpoche, he is the most important figure to followers of Nyingmapa Buddhism and often appears in Buddhist iconography. Here we see him with the two mystic consorts, Mandarawa and Yeshe Tsogyal, and his twenty five closest disciples.*

161 bottom *The* thangkha *primarily came into existence as a tool for meditation. One of the earliest to be displayed adepts that immerse themselves in the Holy Doctrine reproduces a gathering of saints arranged like the petals of the lotus; it dates from the 18th century.*

162 top When the monastery of Sakya was founded, it was built with solid walls and lookout towers at each of the four corners for defensive purposes. The result is a monastery-cum-fort that is unique in Tibet.

162 centre Sakya is a small city that exists around its monastery. At one time, there were two monasteries here: the so-called northern one stood at the base of the hill beyond the small river that forms the valley but only ruins remain. The other, called the southern monastery, is the one commonly known as Sakya.

gardens, the pharmacy etc. so that each may receive his share and the prayer rise from the entire community to "turn the Dharma Wheel".

The message of the Buddha is developped through three turns of the Wheel of Dharma. The first relates to suffering and how it can be overcome; this is united with the second that, with the Perfection of Wisdom, concentrates on the emptiness of phenomena. The third leads to understanding the emptiness of the self and the innate potential in each of us to achieve the state of Buddha, once we have learned how to move beyond our conventional perception of the world. The branch of Buddhism that has spread throughout Tibet is derived from the teachings of Buddha and the Indian masters who founded the Mahayana (the Universal Vehicle). The ideal of the Mahayana is seen in the *bodhisattva,* the individual who has the potential to achieve spiritual liberation but who opts to remain in the phenomenal world to aid all living beings to achieve enlightenment. The teachings of the Mahayana are variously combined with Indian Tantric teachings linked to mystical experience that is realised through rituals and formulas and with the help of a *mandala,* the "circle" that encloses a sacred space and which allows the devotee to visualize and identify himself with the divinity. It is a ceremonial tool and a perfect expression of "Buddhahood" on the path to spiritual liberation from the world of the *samsara;* it allows the individual to transcend both himself and the world, at which time all deceptive distinctions disappear, including the discrimination between *samsara* and *nirvana.*

Symbolised by the golden wheel on the pediment of the monastery together with the deers of Buddha's first discourse, the Dharma is the Doctrine, the supporting element of religious life. It was the historical Buddha, Shakyamuni, who left his message to men. His teachings (which tradition says were collected in "three baskets") and their commentaries translated into the Tibetan language make up the Kanjur and the Tenjur. Their influence is

162 bottom During its maximum splendour in the 13th and 14th centuries, Sakya monastery was the spiritual and political centre of Tibet. Linked to the Yuan court by patronage, the Chinese emperor's spiritual adviser came from Sakya and, in return, the governors of Tibet received the imperial seals.

162-163 The few monks that live in Sakya monastery today are gathered around the altar in the prayer hall. The large drums used to mark the stages of a recitation can be seen at the end of the two pews at the sides of the photograph.

163 bottom left, 163 bottom right
Votive lamps are lit inside the monastery
as a symbol of the light that chases away
the darkness of ignorance. The flames are
fed by the faithful with yak butter which
has been replaced almost everywhere by
ghee, margarine originally from Nepal.

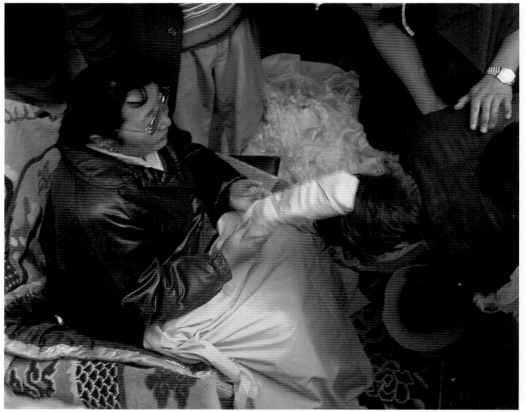

maintained in monasteries through study, recitation and prayers and they are preserved on library shelves in sets of sacred volumes. Patiently copied by an amanuensis or printed using a system of matrices, each book is like a pile of long, loose sheets protected by two wooden covers, often finely illuminated, and wrapped in a length of yellow silk.

The Cultural Revolution consistently attacked these holy texts as the depositories and the symbol of a system that needed to be eliminated; the texts' most valuable parts were taken away to be sold on the antiques market and huge bonfires were made with the rest, together with destructions and killings. Few texts survived, but enough to allow reprinting to start using modern equipment and formats. Recently, photocopying has also been introduced which is decidedly simpler and cheaper to use though its product is much shorter-lived than the handwritten pages of the past. The photocopier might therefore be thought of as a symbol of the impermanence of phenomena that the philosophy of Buddha so often refers to.

164 top The monastery of Samding stands on a rise not far from Lake Yamdrog tsho. Founded by the princess of Gunthang, it follows the Bodong school of Buddhism which enjoyed its maximum glory in the 15th century.

164 centre The 12th Dorje Pamo is the abbess of the convent of Samding. A charismatic and shrewdly political person, she has succeeded in maintaining her role in the convent and promoting its restoration.

164-165 *The art of debating was once exercised in nearly all monasteries but today, with the reduced number of monks and schools, it is only to be heard in the most important centres. This group of monks is debating on the terrace of the Jokhang.*

164 bottom *The recently begun restoration of Samding has reconstructed the buildings, reinstated the effigies of the patron saints and brought back life to a school of philosophy.*

165 bottom *The monastery of Bodong E, not far from Shigatse, is the mother house of the philosophical school of Bodong. As a result of the mediation of Abbess Dorje Pamo, the monks were recently donated the entire works of their founder reprinted in India. It was a moment of great celebration for the whole village.*

166 top left *One of the simplest and most common forms of devotion is the use of the prayer wheel. They usually have painted or engraved symbolic figures and* mantra. *The language and characters are usually Sanskrit which is considered by the people to be the language used by the wise and in religion.*

As so many important books are required just to acquire knowledge, its transmission cannot be reduced to simple scholastic learning. The master/disciple relationship, therefore, is fundamental, not only for the passing on of knowledge, but above all for a personal introduction to the mystery of the spiritual life and the path to enlightenment; this is the song of Marpa, the master, at the time he has to take his leave of Milarepa, his disciple:

"I prostrate myself before you who are full of compassion,
 and I pray.
Contemplating the lives of the masters one sees that even a
 desire for more instruction is a distraction.
Keep the essence of the teaching safe in your heart.
Too many explanations without the essence
Is like many trees without fruit.
Though they are knowledge, they are not the ultimate truth.
To know them all is not the knowing of truth.
Too much elucidation brings not spiritual benefit.
That which benefits the heart is our sacred treasure.
If you wish to be rich, concentrate on this.

166 bottom *A mural of the wheel of life is often present under the entrance porch to monasteries. It is full of symbolic elements with precise references to the forms of existence, the cycle of rebirths and enlightenment. The wheel is held in the mouth of Yama, a demonic figure who personifies death and who wishes to take possession of man. Man, of course, wants to achieve enlightenment and* nirvana *but death aims to prevent this and drag man back to* samsara. *The image of the skull is often present in Buddhist iconography and is a powerful image used to concentrate the mind on the impermanence of human things.*

166-167 *The monks in Samye monastery are busy building a* mandala *of sand. The purpose of this fairly common ritual is to create a three-dimensional* mandala *for use in meditation. It is prepared following a particular ceremony that requires several days of intense collective work.*

167 bottom *During the preparation of the* mandala, *the monk lets differently coloured sand fall, grain by grain, without touching it with his hand and the design is slowly created in every detail. When the radiant construction has been completely finished, the* mandala *is quickly destroyed and the sand thrown into a stream as a sign of the impermanence of things.*

168 top left *Monks usually attend to their spiritual lives but sometimes have to consider material matters. On a feast day, the monks of Trandruk prepare* pakza magu, *balls of white flour that are boiled and flavoured with melted butter, cheese and sugar.*

168 top right *Meditation is one of the indispensable practices of monastic life. The monk sits in the lotus position, closes his eyes, entwines his fingers in the figure of the* mandala *and concentrates on his inner being.*

168 bottom *The large shell that has been brought from far away seas has been decorated and turned into a ceremonial instrument. A long energetic blow coupled with suitable skill produces a deep, arcane sound.*

The Dharma is the skillful means for overcoming mental defilement.
If you wish to be secure, concentrate on it.
A mind that is free from attachments is the Master of Contentment.
If you want a good master, concentrate on this.
The worldly life causes tears; abandon laziness.
A rocky cave in the wilderness was home of your spiritual Father.
A deserted and solitary place is a divine abode.
Mind riding upon mind is a tireless horse.
Your own body is a sanctuary and celestial mansion.
Undistracted meditation and action is the best of all medicine.
To you who have the true aim of Enlightenment
I have given instruction without concealment.
Myself, my instruction and yourself,
The three are placed in your hand, my son.
May they prosper as leaves, branches, and fruit,
Without rotting, scattering, or withering."
That is what he sang, then he placed his hand on my head and exclaimed, "Son, your departure breaks my heart. Impermanence is the mark of all composite things, we can do nothing about it . . ."

The master/disciple relationship developed especially when small groups of disciples started to form around a master, then, when their number increased, they formed a proper monastic community which may have been built around the original cave. Without erasing the tradition of the masters attracted by the solitude of a hermit, the monasteries grew in size and number. Although the direct master/disciple relationship persisted, inside the monastic institutions a complex scholastic system with classes, books, masters and specializations came into being. The level of education in schools was assessed by means of examinations and debates, the latter testing the knowledge of two pupils in a routine of question and answers accompanied by ritual gestures. Debates were widespread in schools and universities where they took place under the strict and benevolent gaze

168-169 In addition to being studied, the Kanjur and Tenjur are also read aloud in some monasteries. Independently of one another, the monks read one of the holy texts from the immense collection as quickly as possible. The purpose of reading fast and aloud is so that the holy words enter the air and produce a vibration that rises to heaven to benefit all living beings.

169 bottom Another activity of the monks is preparing katak which are given to pilgrims so that they might be presented as a sign of veneration. Katak is offered to a god, to a reincarnated lama or to a holy place but may also be presented to a relative, friend or to a guest at the moment of arrival or departure. The monks at work are from Drepung.

170 top, 170 centre Deities and great figures that have risen to achieve a divine role appear in Lamaist Buddhism iconography as aids to visualization and meditation. Placed on a lotus throne, they are reproduced as murals or on thangkha. Here we see Dorje Jigje — the "destroyer of death" — and Padmasambhava with his characteristic sceptre in new paintings in the monastery of Trandruk.

170 bottom This view of the monastic city of Drepung shows several buildings that have been restored. Built by a disciple of Tsongkhapa, it became one of the great universities of the Gelugpa sect that produced the ruling classes of the country.

170-171 Monastic life continues in the restored colleges of Drepung. It may not boast its former splendour and have few resident monks but the citadel can present its face to the world with dignity.

171 bottom The photographs of the 9th and 10th Panchen Lamas have been placed in the glare of the lamps respectively to the left and right of an altar dedicated to Buddha. The pictures are the object of continual worship by the monks and the lay population.

into a corner, the weaker party recognised the superiority of his adversary's position and prostrated himself as a mark of respect. The art of debating is still practised today, though to a lesser extent, in the large monasteries that have succeeded in regenerating themselves.

June 1998. The Bodongpa monastery at Samding near the sacred lake of Yamdrog. In the violent light of the summer solstice at an altitude of 14,500 feet, the large courtyard dominated by the recently rebuilt flight of steps fills with the reddish-brown smudges of the monks. The shaved heads, bare arms and bronzed muscular bodies are the marks of the continuous physical and spiritual exercise of the twenty or so young monks. They sit around one who, standing, puts questions to a companion with elegant gestures and using the vocal rhythms of ritual formulas. His words close with a step forward and a clap of the hands which indicate that his adversary has the floor. From the terrace, the head monk looks on and smiles; it was he with the abbess Dorje Pamo that enabled this monastery to come to life again and continue the tradition of Bodong Chole Namgyal.

Cultivation of the art of the debate is part of the effort that Tibetans are making to keep the roots of their culture alive. At one time, important debates also carried a political significance in which victory could lend weight to the spiritual supremacy of the speaker's patron and in some way increase his political power.

Religious contests sometimes reflected dissension between monasteries and/or between their patrons and, right from its early days, the monastic structure showed itself to be an economic and political force of great importance. The accounts of the founding of Samye tell us that the first abbot of the monastery asked the king, Trisong Detsen, to "assign two hundred families to the temple and three to each monk so that their

of the master and played a determining role in the arguments for the supremacy of one school of thought over another.

The biography of the great master Bodong Chole Namgyal recounts:

"In the middle was the lion throne surmounted by a canopy as beautiful as the wings of a peacock. On it was the master of the doctrine, Chole Namgyal. To the right there was the throne of Yak Mipham, the great preacher of the doctrine, and to the left, the throne of the king. Around them a crowd of scholars was witnessing and evaluating the debate. To commence, the king showing great respect, joined his palms and touched his own forehead to the forehead of the scholars. He said: "Two great masters, like sun and moon, meet here to discuss the holy doctrine. This is a great blessing for the doctrine and I hope it will satisfy all the expectations of their followers. The wish is that the debate be kept within the bounds of the subject". Then Bodong Chole Namgyal began ...".

The debate used to last hours and hours interrupted only occasionally for tea until, forced

172-173 The symbol of Buddhism, the Wheel of Dharma with the deers of Sarnath, is also displayed on the pediment of the assembly room in the monastery of Sera, Tibet's second monastic city. It is a continuous hymn to religion and to the message of the Buddha.

172 bottom left In a citadel like Sera, buildings of minor importance stand in lines interposed by courtyards. The presence of flowers in the windows shows that the place is still active.

172 bottom right The college of Sera je is the largest building in the citadel. Its assembly hall receives light from the large second floor windows shown here from the outside.

work could guarantee the continuance of the monastery". If the quantity of material goods supplied to the first monastery was irrelevant, just a century later at the time of Langdarma, the number of men and assets that the monasteries absorbed was enough to weigh upon spending for the military and defence of the kingdom.

Under the fifth Dalai Lama, the monastic community grew to a gigantic size with a census in 1663 showing there were 1800 monasteries with over 100,000 monks and nuns. The monasteries were autonomous strongholds exempted from paying tax or from providing unpaid feudal labour as they were places for study and exercise that supplied the government with dignitaries and ministers. The immense number of men and women dedicated to religion and the fact that the country's best resources went to the monasteries brought about the progressive weakening of the nation's organizational structure.

As a result of analysis of monastic archives by the researcher Dieter Schuh, "... if at Samye there were 64 monks, subsequent demographic studies show that the number of monks and nuns in the area of Tibetan culture had reached a total that oscillated between 227,000 – 378,000 out of an overall population of between 3-5 millions. In other words, the economic resources used at the time of the empire to maintain 200,000 soldiers in the Tibetan army were later required to maintain the monastic population. ... This transfer of resources had the inevitable consequence of forcing the Tibetan state to neglect important political tasks like defence of

173 bottom The assembly room opens onto a wide court that used to hold all the monks, including those from other colleges that had come to celebrate festivities. A pole stands in the centre of the court to hold the tarchog, *white strips of cloth on which* mantra *are printed.*

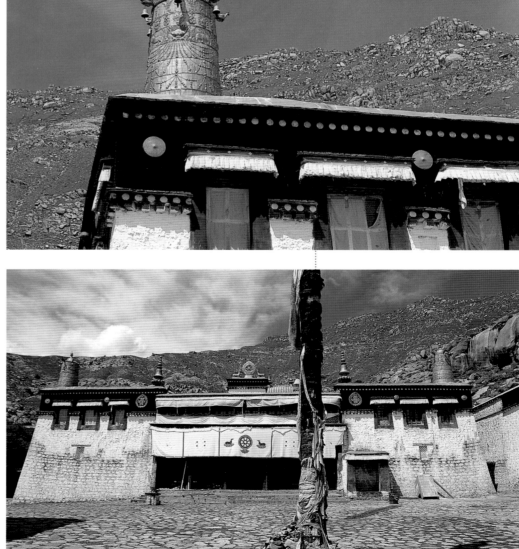

173 top, 173 centre The gyeltsen, *or victory standard, rises grandly above the assembly room at* Sera. Gyeltsen *are made from metal and contain fragments of pages from the holy scriptures.*

*174 top Like Drepung, Sera was also
founded by a disciple of Tsongkhapa. The
altars hold images of the great figures of
Buddhism with special reference to the
Gelugpa sect. This is the great master
Tsongkhapa making the gesture of teaching.*

*174 centre, 174 bottom A lovely shade
of red dominates the large rooms of the
various colleges; it is the reflection in the
altars of the colours of the walls, columns,
butter lamps and even the rugs where the
monks sit. Religious life only occasionally
takes place in these large halls.*

the country. … Indeed, from the time of the fifth
Dalai Lama, Tibet depended militarily and
politically on others, such as the Mongols and
Chinese. Internal disputes and external threats were
resolved by appealing to foreigners. The result was a
general draining of Tibet's sovereignty".

Their walls may have been destroyed or only
partially rebuilt and piles of rubbish may lie where
the goats graze but the monasteries are a continual
presence in Tibet. Created to glorify the Doctrine,
they were founded by masters of philosophy and for
centuries represented the spiritual and material
fulcrum in the life of the whole population.

The layout and dimensions of the monasteries
vary but they tend to reflect the model of the *mandala*
for which the prototype is Samye. The main body of
the building is usually square and has four doors,
one of which is usually kept open. The altar with the
statues of the Buddha and various holy men stand in
the centre with a double line of cushions before
them used by monks during religious ceremonies.
Outside the door, there is a porch usually decorated
with frescoes and steps that lead down into the
courtyard where offices and cells are located if the
ground permits. If the monastery hosted a large
number of monks, cells were also situated in the
small houses around the monastery that were
scattered across the side of the hill like white dice.

No longer able to guarantee maintenance of the
monks, who must therefore be supported by their
families, nowadays the monasteries are obliged to
limit the number of novices. To cover general
expenses, the monks have dreamed up sometimes
ingenious moneymaking schemes: the building up of
a herd of animals from small donations, a return to
traditional Tibetan medicine where the knowledge
exists, the creation of a guest house to be visited by
pilgrims and tourists or the production and sale of
devotional objects such as prayer flags, small statues
or books.

*174-175 The monastic city of Sera
stands on the northern edge of the valley of
Lhasa. The buildings appear to gently
nudge one another gracefully down the
hill. Colleges and cells alternate with tree-
filled courtyards where philosophical
debates still take place today.*

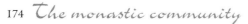

175 bottom left A thangkha depicting Tsongkhapa, the founder, can be seen in the shadows between the columns and the decorations.

175 bottom right The gallery contains statues of famous and less famous figures from the past that carried Buddhism to glory. Religious masters are often shown making the gesture of teaching. This is one of the eight manifestations of Padmasambhava.

176 top Samye was the first Buddhist monastery in Tibet and as such declared itself open to all sects belonging to Nyingmapa Buddhism (non-reformed Buddhism) particularly referred to Padmasambhava.
The symbol with the wheel and the deers is valid for all sects.

176 centre The central body of Samye monastery stands exactly in the middle of the mandala. Its squareness is emphasized where it rises above the first floor terrace.

176-177 Samye complex was built on the model of the mandala of Odantapuri in Bihar in India. The central temple, called Utse, depicts Mount Meru and includes two floors in Tibetan style, one in Chinese style and the topmost in Indian style. The stele of king Trisong Detsen stands in front of the entrance on the left.

Currently, most of the monasteries practise Gelugpa Buddhism but they are only part of a long and glorious series. The school that is traditionally considered the oldest is the Nyingmapa which can be directly traced to the master Padmasambhava, also worshipped as Guru Rinpoche, and to texts from the time of the first diffusion of Buddhism in Tibet. The Nyingmapa only formed a real order in the 11th and 12th centuries as a reaction to, and buffer against, the promoters of the second wave of Buddhism and a large part of their holy texts is made up of those believed to have been hidden by Padmasambhava, his mystical consort and contemporary grand masters. The hidden texts were found and later revealed at certain times by the *tertonpa* – "discoverers of spiritual treasures" – and passed on to Nyingmapa followers. Today initiation to the order must still be conferred on a master/disciple basis. The Nyingmapa practicioners are either monks and live in the monastery or are Tantric masters, who might marry and lead a normal family life. The Nyingmapa tradition is especially

177 top At the four corners of the mandala inside the holy circular enclosure stand four chorten – stupa in Sanskrit – which have recently been restored.

177 centre The corner of the third floor, the one in Chinese style, has now been returned to its full glory. The drawing of a dorje can be seen against the green background of the tower.

177 bottom This is the courtyard surrounding the central body as seen from the terrace on the first floor. The porch around the courtyard opens onto the monks' cells.

178 top The collection of statues at Samye monastery has also been restored. According to ancient models, now the effigies of the gods and famous figures from Buddhist history seen standing in a long line in all the main monasteries have been returned.

178 centre The image of Thangtong Gyalbo, who lived in the 15th century, is frequently found in the gallery. Besides being a religious master, he established Tibetan operatic art and built the iron bridges across the Brahmaputra.

178 bottom The figure of Buddha, particularly in his future manifestation, is also much worshipped at Samye. The photograph shows Maitreya, the Buddha of the future, with his hand raised in the traditional pose of a master teaching.

widespread in the mountains, where monastic institutions and a long curriculum of studies are not easy to organise. Simplified forms of transmission of the teachings from the master to his disciples allow priests to practise religious functions while also leading a normal existence as farmers or animal breeder.

Descendants of those who continued to worship the Tibetan deities rather than Buddhism deem themselves Bonpo. Considered heterodox, they absorbed many Buddhist principles when they organized themselves as an institutionalized religion and used several Buddhist symbols which they inverted. The swastika was an ancient sign of stability drawn by Buddhists with the arms pointing to the right which the Bonpo used with the arms pointing to the left. When walking in the *khora*, the Bonpo followers proceed anti-clockwise and if the holy place is the same for both religions, they will meet the Buddhists coming in the other direction. A great number of Bonpo monasteries and sanctuaries are located in areas that used to belong to the ancient kingdom of Shang Shung, at least according to Bonpo beliefs. Shang Shung remains their principal historical and mythological reference although the two most important Bonpo monasteries are situated in central-western Tibet not far from Shigatse on the north bank of the Brahmaputra.

All the other Buddhist schools of thought go back to religious figures who were protagonists during the second wave of Buddhism. The Sakyapa are followers of Drokmi, an itinerant grand master, one of whose followers founded the monastery of Sakya in 1073; major importance was conferred on the Sakyapa school when its masters became imperial

tutors at the Yuan court in Peking. The Kagyupa are followers of Marpa and Milarepa whose teachings were handed down to generations of disciples that subsequently founded different sects. Of these the Karmapa first introduced the system of reincarnation to Tibet.

During the forty-day period after death, the principle of consciousness of the deceased separates definitively from the body and can be reincarnated in a new living being, inferior if the *karma* has been negative but superior if positive. If, on the other hand, enlightenment has been achieved, the consciousness will be liberated forever from the cycle of rebirths except in the case of a *bodhisattva* who is a

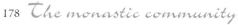

178-179 *The monastic community of Samye is active but only within the limits granted. Numerous youngsters attend the philosophy school and participate in religious ceremonies. So that Samye's religious activities can be carried on, the monks run an nice guest-house beside the monastery.*

179 bottom *The decorated columns and recently renovated drapes are evidence of the attention that this monastery continues to attract and which prompted the large restoration project.*

180 top Monks at Labrang Tashi kyil monastery in the province of Gansu went down to the river bank in a large procession to complete the performance of a special religious ceremony.

180 bottom The monks are wearing the special vestments they reserve for important occasions. The presence of the parasols suggest that a rinpoche (a reincarnated lama) may be on his way. The procession is accompanied by a real band with drums, cymbals and telescopic trumpets (tungchen) which give deep, intense notes.

figure that achieved enlightenment as a human but chooses to be reincarnated to help other living beings. Using a special rite, the *bodhisattva* is able to control separation of the principle of consciousness from the body and its successive reincarnation. The new being carries clear identifying characteristics of its predecessor and a complex criterion of divination and interpretation of the signs exists that allows it to be recognized. This system was used for a long time by the Karmapa and other sects in order to continue transmission of religious and spiritual values embraced by great figures. When the system was adopted by the Gelugpa sect, it was used to decide the succession of the Dalai Lama, the person considered to be the emanation of Chenresi from a religious point of view and the country's political guide.

Bodongpa and Jonangpa are schools of thought that enjoyed glory during the 14th-16th centuries

180-181 *Next to the* stupa *in the courtyard at Gyantse, the large silk* thangkha *embroidered by the monks is being unrolled. This ceremony is very popular with Tibetans but only occurs on a few important occasions. Slowly, the monks unroll the fabric to reveal the face of Buddha. This photograph was taken in 1981.*

181 bottom *Monks play the* gyalin — *a sort of oboe with a characteristic and unusual sound to the western ear — to announce the arrival of the* rinpoche *and on other important occasions.*

182-183 Trandruk monastery is one of the twelve temples built by Princess Wencheng to subdue the she-demon hidden below Tibetan soil. Each temple was a "nail" to hold the demon down and the location of Trandruk corresponds to the left shoulder.

182 bottom Trandruk monastery is a destination for Tibetan pilgrims but it is also visited by the new generation of tourists-cum-pilgrims as it is situated at the beginning of the Yarlung valley not far from the tombs of the kings. The famous eight symbols of Buddhism are shown in pairs on the wall of a courtyard.

bringing the Dharma to western Tibet. The Kadampa believed themselves restorers of a more disciplined religious tradition compared with the system that had been corrupted in the chaos following the collapse of the Tibetan empire. They believed that whoever had taken vows had to maintain his faith and, above all, had to dispense with the aberrant Tantric practices which, rather than leading to enlightenment, could only keep one within the infernal cycle of rebirths. In the 14th century, the grand master Tsongkhapa welcomed the strict line taken by the Kadampa and founded what became the Gelugpa school, or the "virtuous ones". The reform was hugely successful and, with the ascension to power of the fifth Dalai Lama, the Gelugpa became the most widespread sect in Tibet. They assimilated monasteries of other schools of thought and everywhere imposed the austerity of renunciation. Their monasteries and monks increased in number while the monastic cities they built around Lhasa assumed importance and political influence.

The monastic cities were built as centres for religious study and played the role of universities that produced the members of the ruling class of abbots, masters and ministers. The cities were organized around a group of economically and organizationally independent colleges, each headed by an abbot appointed by the Dalai Lama, and educated an incredible number of monks. Each college owned assets which produced income that was used to pay for the huge festivals necessary to ensure the spiritual well-being of the people. An area set aside outside the walls was used for "heavenly funerals"; in this place such ceremonies are still performed to judge by a story told by a young man from Lhasa:

"My aunt lay dead in her cell when the lama read the signs: it was necessary to celebrate a heavenly funeral. We came to an agreement with the monks and at the set time we went to the place. The vultures were circling low overhead and made me uneasy. The body was placed in a ceremonial

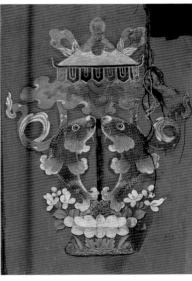

but the power of the Gelugpa reduced them to minor importance. The Jonangpa had their centre at Puntsholing on the right bank of the Brahmaputra; they were considered heretics for their unique doctrinal views on the essence of emptiness but they were also unfortunate in being supported by the king of Tsang. When the king was defeated, the Jonangpa monks were persecuted and most of their monasteries transformed into Gelugpa centres. The Bodongpa were politically less committed so experienced the transformation less severely, losing only some of their monasteries.

The Kadampa, the followers of the "pure word", were fundamental to the history of the second wave of Buddhism, as they were descended from the great master Atisha who arrived from India in 1042

183 These pictures show the various symbols of Buddhism: the white shell that sounds in celebration of Buddha's enlightenment stands over the infinite knot that symbolizes the intertwining of love and harmony (top); the parasol that protects the image of Buddha stands over the two golden fish leaping out of the water to indicate liberation from the circle of life (centre); the lotus flowers that represent Buddha's purity and compassion emerge from the container of great treasures, i.e. the jewels of enlightenment (bottom right); and the victory standard that celebrates the triumph of Buddhist wisdom is placed above the eight-spoked wheel that symbolizes the Eight Noble Truths, commonly known as the Wheel of Dharma (bottom left).

184 bottom left The statues have recently been remade on traditional lines. This is Maitreya in the classical pose of blessing and teaching.

184 bottom right Songtsen Gampo, the Tibetan king that championed Trandruk's construction, is considered highly in the monastery. Here he is shown in a statue flanked by his two wives, the Chinese Wencheng and the Nepalese Birikuti. These statues too are modern.

184-185 Trandruk monastery was constructed at the time of Songtsen Gampo and later expanded by Trisong Detsen. It has always been considered of major importance. It was heavily damaged during the Cultural Revolution, but a large restoration project was recently undertaken.

circle. *The celebrant removed the scalp with a small iron hook, took the knife, sank the blade into the ritual spot and began to cut. Then he moved away to make room for the vultures who swooped down to eat the meat and skin. The remainder was cut to pieces and mixed with* tsampa, *the head was cracked open with a large stone and then all was left once more to the heavenly patrons until nothing remained. I was still a boy but it was a duty I could not avoid and it has given me much occasion to reflect on the impermanence of human life...".*

There are four monastic cities in Tibet: Drepung, Sera and Ganden near Lhasa are the traditional "three seats"; the fourth, Tashilhunpo, is at Shigatse, Tibet's second largest city.

The clean white buildings of Drepung ("pile of rice") stand to the north of Lhasa where the plateau begins to slope. The city was founded by a disciple of Tsongkhapa and immediately grew to enormous size until it was able to accommodate ten thousand monks. Before the Potala was built, Drepung was the temporal seat of the Dalai Lama and the definitive seat of the remains of the second, third and fourth reincarnations in their precious urns. Drepung was marginally affected during the Cultural Revolution and many of its buildings remained intact and now, mostly renovated, it is home to about five hundred monks. A well-defined route of rooms, corridors and stairs gives the visitor a fine example of what monastic organization used to be like.

Sera is the second monastic city and is also located on the north side of the valley. It was founded by a disciple of Tsongkhapa with as many as five colleges, one of which was dedicated to the instruction of itinerant monks from remote areas of the country. At one time there were five thousand monks dwelling there; now there are only a few hundred. The philosophical school is still active but sometimes the monks are obliged to "put on a show" for tourists.

185 top Small altars and niches with religious symbols are objects of devotion by more than the monks whose job it is to look after them. Constantly attended to, their butter lamps are permanently alight.

185 centre The details too are interesting even if they have been recreated. Here we see two crossed dorje *and two swastikas. The* dorje *is the vajra, Sanskrit symbol for a diamond, while the swastika - yungdrung in Tibetan — is the ancient symbol of stability. The Bonpo draw their* yungdrung *rotating to the left while, for the Buddhists, they rotate to the right.*

185 bottom Following its restoration, the assembly hall has been ornamented once more. Even if it appears empty in the picture, the room is again being used for ceremonies. The monastery is kept active by a small group of monks, evidence of whom can be seen in the few things they have left on the cushions.

186 top The monastery of Tashilhunpo at Shigatse was founded in 1447 by a disciple of Tsongkhapa. Thanks to the influence of the Panchen Lama, it was spared by the Cultural Revolution and its temples and chapels still boast their ancient ornaments.

Worn out by all their picture taking, the foreigners arrive in a courtyard shaded by willow trees. Here, in front of the implacable eyes of the telephoto lenses, a group of monks tiredly exhibit the art of debating. Afterwards, the monks sit on the grass amused and amazed as they watch the strange visitor, with a bundle of small denomination notes in his hand, attempting to re-enact the ancient practice of kugye *that he has learned of elsewhere. In the background, an old monk smiles but his lined face betrays a slight expression of regret.*

Ganden lies in the Kyichu valley 30 miles or so east of the capital. Founded by Tsongkhapa himself, two years before his death, Ganden was the first Gelugpa monastery and has been the heart of this philosophy ever since. It is here that the founder's remains, his hermitage, the room he died in and his tomb can be seen. Built at over 13,000 feet in an amphitheatre open to the east, the citadel is made up of large, solid buildings and an infinite number of smaller constructions such as monks' cells, temples, holy walls and reliquaries. The ritual route, the *khora*,

financial or other means in their attempt to piece back together the fragments of their existence. A huge reconstruction project was later undertaken which gave back to the complex part of its ancient splendour in just a few years.

The fourth monastic city is Tashilhunpo, the seat of Panchen Lama. It stands on the north side of the city of Shigatse at the foot of a hill on which festoons of prayer flags fly. This monastery was founded by the disciple of Tsongkhapa who was posthumously recognized as the first Dalai Lama. The importance of the city grew when the fifth Dalai Lama recognized the abbot of Tashilhunpo –

186 centre A powerful religious symbol, the seat of the Panchen Lama is an object of great popular devotion. Many people can be seen each dawn performing their religious rituals.

186 bottom The mortal remains of the Panchen Lamas are kept at Tashilhunpo in large mausoleums with golden roofs that stand higher than all the other buildings. The mausoleum in the photograph is the resting place of the remains of the 10th Panchen Lama.

186-187 Ten Panchen Lamas so far have guided Tashilhunpo. On their deaths, the large monastic city has taken their remains and placed them in magnificent individual mausoleums.

passes around the complex like a narrow path between rugged slopes and sheer walls of rock. Incense-burners are lit in order by the pilgrims in the small prayer stations along the way and send white perfumed whorls of smoke skyward. Caves and recesses dug in the rock offer deviations with short mazelike stretches that represent the different stages of the *bardo* – the gap that separates death from the next rebirth – from which the devotee exits a little bruised and dirty but spiritually renewed. Such symbolism made Ganden a particular target during the 1959 revolt and the Cultural Revolution, when it was reduced to a ruin. Restoration was begun discreetly by a group of voluntary workers without

*187 top Even the courtyards of
Tashilhunpo are surrounded by colonnades
that provide a covered walking area.
The photograph shows one such area
on the first floor that allows spectators
to attend ceremonies taking place
in the courtyard.*

*187 centre Devotion to the Panchen Lama
still continues in the monastery of
Tashilhunpo. The photograph of the 10th
Panchen Lama, who died in 1989, is still
found on all the altars.*

188 top left A katak *has been placed on the arms of this statue of Maitreya and a rosary in his hands.*

188 top right *One of the great masters of the Gelugpa sect sits on the large throne among golden decorations and coloured strips.*

188 bottom left *The great master and magician Padmasambhava has a polymorphous appearance in Buddhist iconography. He has eight manifestations, one of which is this terrifying expression.*

of whom he was a disciple – as the emanation of Öpagme, the Buddha of infinite light, and gave him the title of Panchen Lama, Grand Master.

The relationship between the two greatest religious authorities in Tibet was conceived as that of a master and his disciple, moreover each had to recognize the reincarnation of the other and assist him spiritually during childhood, so it was a relationship that over the centuries experienced moments of harmony but also of rivalry. For example, rather than follow the Dalai Lama into exile in the 1950s, the tenth Panchen Lama preferred to remain in Tibet and mediate with the Chinese authorities. At first they regarded him favourably but at the beginning of the 1960s he presented them with a secret report in which he criticized the regime and which Mao referred to as the "poisoned arrow".

Regardless of the difficulties he incurred, he spared no efforts towards the end of his earthly life during the era of openness promoted by Deng Xiao-ping in order to revitalize Tibetan culture and protect the natural environment. He died in in Shigatse on 10 January 1989, which led to the difficult problem of recognising the eleventh Panchen Lama. His body was taken with great honour to Tashilhunpo where a magnificent *stupa* was built for him next to that of his predecessors. Tashilhunpo was not damaged during the Cultural Revolution

188 bottom right and 189 bottom
The statues and thangkha *representing the gods and figures of Buddhism are for the most part of recent manufacture. Sometimes what was destroyed is completely replaced but often additions overlay ancient remains, as in wall paintings, with results that are often devastating.*

188-189 After death, the body of the great lamas is mummified using salt and essences. When the process is complete, the body is placed in the chorten *in the centre of the mausoleum while the salt is distributed to the faithful to be kept as a relic. This is the* chorten *of the 4th Panchen Lama.*

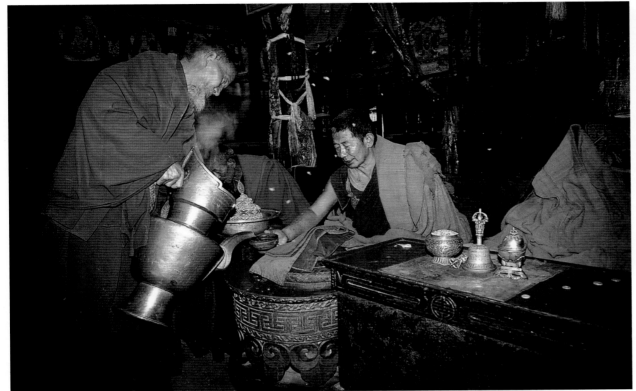

and today is the only monastic city left practically intact. Its golden roofs are visible from afar and decorations, statues and ritual objects adorn the tombs of the Panchen Lama. It may be a mausoleum but it is also alive; Tashilhunpo is home to groups of monks who read the words of Buddha aloud unceasingly day and night.

A murmur of singing, chanting and shouting voices echoes down the corridor of the last palace. It sounds like a storm at sea but also like a strange song sung by many voices, each of which is following its own rhythm within a common thought. When the door opens, the monks can be seen through the smoke of the incense; some are seated, others standing, all are reading. The shelves of the library surround the monks with the infinite volumes of the Kanjur and the Tenjur. Their voices chant the word of Buddha uninterruptedly so that the flow of invocation and benediction between heaven and earth rises for the benefit of all living beings.

190 The gigantic statue of Maitreya (Jampa in Tibetan) is one of Tashilhunpo's greatest attractions. Lined with gold, it was made by the 9th Panchen Lama and placed in a purpose-built chapel. The statue is 85 feet high and requires a flight of stairs over several floors to view the various parts of the body properly.

191 top left The monks' lives are lived amongst the thousands of statues that adorn the many altars. Prayer hours alternate with rest periods when salted butter tea arrives from the kitchens in thermos flasks or in the huge copper urn.

191 top right Thangkha are also hung in the altars displaying Buddhism's greatest saints. Whether made a long time ago or since the Cultural Revolution, they have the same purpose of aiding worship.

191 centre There are countless images of Tsongkhapa, the master whose reforms planted the seed of the new monastic organization. He was also the master that was posthumously nominated the first Dalai Lama.

191 bottom The rooms and altars in Tashilhunpo are also decorated with strips and cylinders of silk and brocade. Hung from the beams or resting on the columns, their purpose is to accompany the mind on its journey of visualization.

192 Tsurpu monastery stands 44 miles north of Lhasa and is the mother-house of the Karmapa sect, a branch of the larger Kagyupa family. Here too, the large silk thangkha with the embroidered picture of Buddha surrounded by religious masters and protectors is unrolled on important festivals such as Losar (New Year) or Sagadawa (the commemoration of the birth, death and enlightenment of Buddha).

193 top, 193 bottom left The celebrations include the holy dance, the cham, in which monks masked as gods recreate episodes and variants of the ancient theme of the struggle between good and evil.

193 bottom right The Karmapa is one of the seven oldest sects. Official recognition of the principle of reincarnation originally came from the Karmapa and was later adopted by the other sects. Currently, their leader is the 17th reincarnation; he is a young, smiling and charismatic lama that enjoys recognition even by the Chinese authorities.

194 bottom To reduce the tension of the spectators between pieces, atsara — *a kind of clown — come on stage to entertain the public. Atsara are grotesque masks of Indian masters and saints.*

194-195 Holy dances are very common in Tibetan monasteries. The pictures show them in the monastery of Katok in east Tibet. Holy dances are a sort of ritual in which the divinity evoked with meditation is represented by an actor wearing a mask. Texts handed down across the generations are adapted for representation by the monks.

195 centre The dances are accompanied by the sound of drums played by musicians seated in a row. All monks not taking part in the show are enthusiastic spectators for the several days that the ceremony generally lasts.

195 bottom Preparation of the costumes is a complex business that requires a great deal of skill. Made from wood and papier-mâché and painted, the masks are kept and renewed when necessary and the monastery is proud of its patrimony.

195 top The masks, including those of animals, were created to make visible the gods that are the fruit of the human mind. Only when the initiate succeeds in overcoming them does he understand that in fact they do not exist. The masks are worn by monks dressed up in coloured clothes.

196 bottom The clothes worn for large ceremonies are magnificent and adorned with heavy symbols. As always, the dominant colours are red and yellow, the colours of light.

196-197 A ritual using sacred weapons is celebrated in the monastery of Tsa Sa in Kham. The ritual had probably already been introduced from India at the time of Padmasambhava to "pacify the soil" for the construction of Samye monastery.

197 top and centre Arms are also used in the holy dances that represent the struggle between good and evil; one is the phurba, *a three-bladed dagger made from metal or wood. The dagger is loaded with energy and is considered a symbol of interior knowledge. Another instrument is the* dri — sword — *which is used to cut the knots of ignorance and attachment.*

198 top right Seriously damaged during the Cultural Revolution, the monastery of Rongbuk has recently undergone a reasonable restoration project. The woman in the picture is spinning the large new prayer wheel.

199 This photograph shows the restored chorten of Rongbuk — the emblem of the Buddhist religion — and the north wall of Everest, considered the Great Mother of the Continents: two powerful symbols of a piety that does not dim.

198 top left The monastery of Rongbuk stands at an altitude of 16,000 feet at the feet of the north wall of Everest. It was built at the start of this century on the site of an ancient hermitage with the contribution of all the inhabitants of the valley. Rongbuk follows the Nyingmapa philosophy that gave rise to the monasteries of Solu and Khumbu on the southern slopes of Everest.

198 bottom left, 198 bottom right Of the 100 monks and nuns that used to live there (mostly nuns), only 15 or so were left but since restoration, their number has increased to forty. To permit their survival, they have created a small guest-house where they welcome tourists and passing climbers in a simple but hospitable manner.

The monastic community

Sacred mountains

and popular devotion

200 top The ancient cults prior to Buddhism considered Nyenchen Tanglha — a 20,000-foot mountain covered with snow that stands over Lake Namtsho — to be the patron god of the tribes that lived at its feet. When the tribes were subjected by the Tibetan kings, the mountain was "decapitated" by Yarlha Shampo — the mountain deity of the adversaries — which placed the "head" at its own feet.

200 top left Yarlha Shampo, the mountain deity of the Tibetan kings, stands at the bottom of the Yarlung valley. It was the forefather of the great king Songtsen Gampo that conquered the lands that "belonged" to Nyenchen Tanglha, cut off the mountain's head and subjected its peoples.

"When the first Tibetan king, Nyatri Tsempo, descended onto Lhari Gyangdo, Mount Rirab bowed nine times … the king descended to earth and was prince of all that is under the heavens; he reigned in the centre of the sky, in the middle of the earth, in the heart of the continent, on the girdle of snow and on all the rivers. The country was excellent … of all the rivers, the Yarchu is the bluest, the Yarlha Shampo is the god of the highest peaks". This myth given in the ancient Tibetan chronicle of Dunhuang was drawn on again by later tradition and continued by detailing the events of a successor, the king-god Drigum, who arrogantly challenged his subjects from the castle of Yumbu Lagang. Everyone was afraid and only one minister accepted the challenge but he artfully managed to induce the proud king to carry the bodies of two dead animals on his back that were supposed to fill him with an immense strength. Instead, they caused the king to be impure which removed him from the favour of his protective deities. Vulnerable during the magic struggle, the king severed the cord of light that linked him to heaven and he fell dead. The kingdom passed into the hands of the minister but the queen did not cease to invoke the ancestral divinities until the mountain deity Yarlha Shampo appeared to her in the form of a white yak. From their union, a son, Rulakye, was born who killed the usurper and restored the Tibetan kingdom.

The ancient myth reaffirms both the divine origin of the royal Tibetan lineage and the fundamental role of mountains in the cosmogonic configuration of Tibet. The mountains are not only the abodes of the gods but gods themselves that give legitimacy to rulers, govern the existence of men and are respected and worshipped. The ceremonies concerning sacred mountains are very ancient and precede the introduction of Buddhism into Tibet. According to the researcher Samten Karmay, ancestral myths recount that when Nyatri Tsempo descended from heaven, his divine forefather ordered him to "celebrate the *sang* rituals in front of him to purify the path". *Sang* means purification and the ritual was supposed to restore the

200 bottom left Yarlha Shampo was also worshipped in its form as a white rider on a white yak, as represented in this thangka.

200 bottom As with many other ancestral divinities, popular belief has attributed a terrifying image to Yarlha Shampo which is only shown during particular festivals.

201 Mani-walls , i.e. piles of stones inscribed with mantra in front of which the faithful prostrate themselves, are one of the most common manifestations of Tibetan devotion. This mani-wall is on the bank of the river Brahmaputra.

202-203 *The castle of Yumbu Lagang was built in the Yarlung valley for king Nyatri Tsempo, a mythical figure who is supposed to have been the first to descend from heaven down a cord of light onto the ancestral mountain.*

202 bottom left *Completely destroyed during the Cultural Revolution, the castle has since been rebuilt on the lines of the ancient version. With the diffusion of Buddhism, the fort took on the appearance of a temple and altars and statues were placed in its chapels.*

202 bottom right The ground floor chapel is dedicated to the great figures that created the Tibetan kingdom: the kings Nyatri Tsempo, Songtsen Gampo, Trisong Detsen and several of their ministers. All the statues are of recent manufacture.

203 top The soaring castle contains three chapels in all, built one on top of another. Butter lamps are lit in front of the statues and religious symbols as signs of devotion.

203 centre This statue of Buddha Sakyamuni is kept in one of the many chapels in the castle and is a faithful copy of the one made at the time of Songtsen Gampo.

203 bottom One of the statues represents Thonmi Sambhota, the minister that went to India in search of writing and returned with Tibetan characters. He is depicted with books in hand and a quill holder on his belt.

officiated by monks.

Dense white whorls of smoke rise from the crackling twigs of juniper and wrap themselves around the faded colours of the prayer flags. Groups of valley-dwellers are clustered on the walls of the ancient crystal palace carefully leaving space in the centre for the monks. Seated on the old square stones, the monks celebrate the ancient sang *ceremony. Towards the end, one of them takes a handful of rolled up prayer flags and passes them repeatedly through the smoke murmuring* mantra. *Then he approaches the ruins of the palace and, with the help of the onlookers, he adds the new prayer flags to the others and, in doing so, suddenly brings the colours of the setting to life. Nearly a thousand feet below, the freezing river crosses the recently ploughed fields like a ribbon of light. The distant and evanescent peak of Mount Everest briefly appears away to the south. All around the setting, the tips of four snowy mountains rear above the bare hills that encircle the valley. They are the mountain deities that stand like pillars to the north, south, east and west of the* mandala *in which the village, monastery and mountain of Shekar are the centre.*

The Shekar is one of the innumerable *mandala* to be found across Tibet. The *mandala* is a ritual aid to meditation, an inspirational aid to architecture and an

harmony between men and the godhead. The *sang* ritual is accompanied by the recitation of a text which evokes the ancient struggle in which the gods defeated the demons. Prayer flags, an integral part of the ritual, are sometimes small rectangles of coloured paper thrown into the air but often rectangular scraps of material in the five basic colours to be hung on pointed sticks or tree branches. Whichever form is chosen, the prayer flag always has certain symbols printed on it with a wooden printing block. The central image is of the horse of the wind which is an expression of the vital force while animal symbols in each corner refer to the ancestral clans of Tibet: the lion, tiger, eagle and dragon. Some *mantra* were also added at later times (a *mantra* is a Buddhist prayer of Sanskrit origin) which officially made the flags a part of the new religion. *Sang* rituals are usually celebrated by laymen although the ceremony is sometimes

204 top A pilgrim prostrates himself full length in front of Mount Kailash. It is not rare for pilgrims to make the entire circuit around the holiest mountain in the world in this fashion.

204 centre Kailash is an ancestral mountain too. Legend says that Tönpa Shenrab, the founder of the Bonpo religion, descended onto the mountain from heaven. Bonpo combined many of the ancient local cults in the country, especially in the area of the ancient kingdom of Shang Shung, but only assumed its current form in the 11th century.

educational aid to interpretation of the sacred countryside; on Tibetan soil it has been further endowed with pre-existing sacred components. Popular tradition considers geographical features in key points, above all mountains, as mountain-gods and the owners of the land on which they stand. Local beliefs relating to the creation of Tibet consider the mountain deities to be concrete entities related by kinship or subjection that reflect existing, or previously existing, relationships of power between different communities. The leader of a Tribe is the "son" of the ancestarl mountain, from whom he receives legitimation and power. The most important "son" was obviously Nyatri Tsempo, the king who descended from heaven to Mount Yarlha Shampo. Besides being an ancestral mountain, Yarlha Shampo is one of the nine mountain deities that protect the lands conquered by the Tibetan kings which formed the first nucleus of the kingdom. They were among the opponents of Buddhism subjected by Padmasambhava and in the edict that declared Buddhism to be the state religion, Trisong Detsen invoked the nine mountain deities as witnesses to the pact.

The mountain deities can appear in many different guises; besides being mountains, they are depicted on

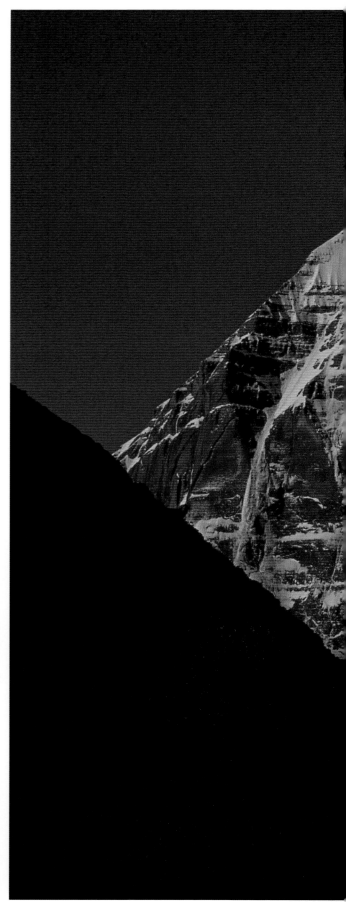

thangka or in frescoes in the form of wild animals, such as tigers or wild yak, but their most frequent image is that of a horseman. Each god on horseback fends off against enemies, fights injustice and has his own colour that is associated with his mountain. Many are white horsemen of which the most important is Nyenchen Tanglha, one of the nine mountain deities linked to the origins of the Tibetan kingdom. It was the time of the kings just before Songtsen Gampo and in the northern areas the tribes living at the feet of Nyenchen Tanglha were joined around a leader. At a certain point betrayal and internal dissent brought to a radical change of the situation and the Tibetan king of Yarlung became

the sovereign of the whole region. The mountain deity in which the local tribes had identified themselves was decapitated - Nyenchen Tanglha has a flat peak - and his head was placed at the feet of Yarlha Shampo, the ancestral god of Tibetan kings, where it can be seen now. The removal of heads, arms, legs and entrails of mountain deities is not rare in the local stories which probably refer to ancient struggles when one tribe was defeated and its land taken. Subjection was symbolized by the part of the mountain removed — gullies, canyons, saddles — that were then placed at the feet of the victorious mountain — represented by swellings, towers or pinnacles.

Not only mountain-rulers but mountain-ministers figure in Tibetan creation beliefs; for example, Mount Makalu (Jobo- lönpo in Tibetan) is the minister to

204-205 Often associated with Mount Meru (the axis mundi*), Mount Kailash is considered to be the centre of the universe. Ascetics and mystics have spent years meditating at its feet, making the area even holier with the traces of their presence. With the exceptions of Tönpa Shenrab, who descended from heaven, and Milarepa, who ascended to the summit on a ray of light, no-one has ever set foot on its snows.*

204 bottom and 205 bottom Visiting Kailash is the realization of a life's dream for many Tibetans. The route around the mountain lies at a very high altitude, is freezing cold and has no shelters for the night. Pilgrims, sometimes very young, travel alone or with their families. Nearly all travel on foot though sometimes accompanied by a yak which carries provisions and, if necessary, the youngest children.

Mount Everest. Descending eastwards down its large crest, we find Surra, the mountain deity of the community that lives in the northern Himalayan valleys. He is depicted as a black, proud and impressive horseman but he is an irascible god that was only transformed into a defender of Buddhism in recent times, and who actually required animal sacrifices as late as a few decades ago. In 1922, when Colonel Howard Bury, the first European, entered the valleys north of Everest and Makalu, he said he found a village that had just been abandoned following a terrible epidemic sent by the god who had been offended by an impious gesture. Today Sakeding is a collection of crumbling and deserted buildings infested by weeds that lies in a clearing in front of the frozen and imperturbable sacred mountain. Surra is the minister of Gangmar, the red horseman who protects the lords that wisely governed the south lands from Everest as far as the Brahmaputra from their crystal palace on the peak of Mount Shekar. The modest Mount Gangmar was surrounded by a great court, part of which was Sichun, the yellow horseman that towers just a little north of Everest. Related to Gangmar was Tashi Ombar, the blue horseman who protects not only land but also the Bodongpa tradition of Buddhism. Also related to Gangmar is the mountain deity Takyong, the protector of horses, who for centuries was the spiritual and material guide to the princes of Porong. A prophecy remembered by

their descendants who fled abroad says that the Porong dynasty was supposed to continue for as long as Takyong was covered with snow. Perhaps it is also because of global warming that the white tip has been missing for some years...

The mountain deity is often associated in popular creation beliefs with the lake-goddess. The two form a dyad – to use the Greek expression applied by scholar John Bellezza – the concept of which has existed among the nomadic people since time immemorial. It was on this dyad that Buddhism overlaid its own concept of *yab yum* represented by the image of a god sexually united with his consort. There are three dyads in the Chang Thang which are, from east to west: Mount Nyenchen Tanglha with Lake Namtsho, Mount Targo with Lake Dangra Yumtsho and Mount Kailash with Lake Manosarovar.

207 top, 207 centre Not only the famous mountains are sacred. In remote areas, the people still identify with the mountain deities. One of these is the community of Porong in the region of Mount Zangla (top) while Kang Ponchen (centre) protects the community of Lhabuk. The two groups have been in permanent conflict over grazing rights. Local legends recount that one day the two mountain deities came to blows and that Kang Ponchen decapitated his adversary and took the head away in the form of a pointed spur. Headless and disembowelled, Mount Zangla was left with a flat summit and many channels of water rushing down its slopes. The boundaries of the grazing rights have recently been revised by the Chinese administration but left no-one happy.

207 bottom Lake Manosarovar is the largest sacred lake in western Tibet. Its clear and bright coloured waters are associated with the sun and the forces of light. In combination with Mount Kailash, it forms the most famous of the Tibetan dyads in which the mountain represents the male element and the lake its female counterpart.

206 The trip around Kailash takes three or four days walk even if some Tibetans are capable of completing it in a single day. It is said that one khora around Kailash will purify one's sins but 108 will lead straight to the path to nirvana.

206-207 Rakshas tal is one of the two large freshwater lakes in the region of Mount Kailash. It receives its waters via a channel from Lake Manosarovar which lies at a slightly higher level. The dark colour of its waters mean it is associated with the moon and the forces of darkness.

Nyenchen Tanglha is the cropped peak half covered with ice directly north of Lhasa that in Tibetan mythology was transported by the Tibetan kings and placed at the feet of Yarlha Shampo. At about 23,000 feet high, the mountain is the tallest in the chain of the same name and the sacred consort of Lake Namtsho. The lake was glacial in origin and contains fresh water, which is a rarity in Tibet. As with the mountains, each lake is both the seat of the goddess and the goddess herself.

The Targo is a chain of eight peaks in the very centre of the Chang Thang that provides a necessary source of local drinking water. It is situated not far away from the city of Kyung dzong, one of the ancient capitals of the kingdom of Shang Shung.

208 top For centuries the valley that leads to the monastery of Rongbuk has been travelled by ascetics and mystics in search of the path to enlightenment in the mountains. Numerous "stations" are to be found on this sacred path where pilgrims pause to pray in front of mani-walls and perhaps too to refresh themselves.

208 centre When a Tibetan traveller reaches the top of a pass, he places a stone on the pile. Then he hangs a katak or a prayer flag and prays to the gods aloud.

208 bottom In eastern Tibet, long strips of cotton on which mantra are printed are hung around a pole as prayers to the gods. With time, the rain and wind reduce the strips until they disappear completely.

208-209 A large standard has been hoisted on Pang la Pass between Dingri and the Rongbuk valley. Surrounded by old katak, the Potala is a potent symbol for all Tibetans. The fog, not rare on this pass, obscures the stunning view of four massive mountains: Makalu, Everest, Cho Oyu and Shisha Pangma.

Deep, salty and enclosed, Lake Dangra is Targo's lake-consort. The beneficent form of the goddess "resides in a castle suffused with turquoise light" as opposed to her terrifying image which has a black serpent's body.

The third dyad is better known. Despite being only 21,820 feet high, Mount Kailash has a bright snowy peak that has earned it the name of "Jewel of Snow". Buddhist cosmology identifies Kailash as Mount Meru, the great mythological mountain that is the *axis mundi* and which exercises an unequalled force of attraction. For the Hindus, the mountain is the throne of Shiva, for the Buddhists it is the abode of Samvara (the transposition of Shiva in Tantric Buddhism) while for the Bonpo it was the spiritual centre of Shang Shung. Kailash was where Milarepa had a famous competition with a Bonpo master in the

209 top Prayer flags are derived from the ancient cult of mountain deities but have been incorporated into the official Buddhist religion. They are known as lungta or "horses of the wind" and are rectangular pieces of cloth coloured in the centre that always show an image of a horse encircled by mantra. Even when they have been almost destroyed by the weather, they cannot be removed but must be left until they are completely worn away.

210 *The rosary is an individual religious practice that is common to all social classes. The crown is made up of 108 beads that are moved slowly as* mantra *are recited.*

211 top left *Prayer bands get greyer with time until they become dark like the rocks: they simbolize the return to the earth.*

211 top right *Mantra engraved on mani-walls may seem almost eternal but they too are subject to the law of transience of matter: with time the engravings will get lost in the surface of the rock.*

211 centre *Menri stands in central Tibet north of the Brahmaputra and is one of the most prestigious Bonpo monasteries. The Bonpo are organized with rules and systems of teaching that reflect the influence of the Gelugpa sect.*

211 bottom *Rituals to stop hail or to summon rain are part of the ancient popular religion. Traditionally celebrated by local priests of different persuasions, they have now become tasks to be performed by the head monk of a monastery.*

Mapam Yumtsho) is another of the few freshwater lakes in Tibet with waters that are associated with the sun and light. Hindus believe that the lake was created by the mind of Brahma. In Buddhist tradition, Maya, the queen and mother of Buddha, was brought here by the gods for a ceremonial bath shortly before the birth of her son.

The mountains of the dyads are still respected and worshipped and their *khora* are deemed pilgrimages to be completed with devotion. The trip around the perimeter of the lakes or mountains requires several weeks of walking, or several months if *chak* are

12th century.

At a certain moment, Mila and his adversary decided to resolve the question with a competition of magic powers: the winner would be the one who first reached the peak of the sacred mountain using any method at all. On the appointed day, the master banged on the ritual drum with which he called the gods during the ceremonies and sped off. Mila, on the other hand, stayed calm and meditated in the blue light of dawn, then, when the first ray of sunshine struck the golden tip of the mountain, he attached himself to the ray and went to the top of the mountain at the speed of light.

The figure of Milarepa is linked to Mount Kailash's eastern valley where, it is said, he lived for eleven years; the western valley, on the other hand, is associated most of all with Padmasambhava who lived there in a cave. Lake Manosarovar (in Tibetan

212 top and centre The epic of Gesar is one of the most typical manifestations of Tibetan popular devotion. His deeds and their hundreds of variants are sung, described and recounted. Festivals requiring great preparation are also held in his honour.

212 bottom The festivals include dancing which is especially popular with all the people. The men wear their best brocaded chupa, traditionally edged with the skin of a tiger or snow leopard, and the indispensable felt hat.

performed, but anyone can complete them: laymen who want to accumulate merit in order to shorten the number of their rebirths and *yogin* for whom the pilgrimage is a part of their journey towards illumination. The physical exercise is an integral part of the journey as the rarefied air demands great physical effort while the sense of immense space, the unspoilt surroundings and the strong sunlight all contribute to purifying the body and mind. The devotee recites *mantra* and performs the required rituals as he makes his journey around the mountain or lake; he is enraptured by the ecstatic vibrations he experiences that match those emitted by the land on which generations of spiritual masters have left their mystical mark. Almost all sacred places have a "pilgrim guide" (the *neyik*) that describes the route, the holiest places, traces that may have been left by holy men or mystics, the "still hidden holy texts", the sacred waters in which to purify oneself, and places to burn incense, to prostrate oneself and hang prayer flags. In these guides, travelling companions are referred to as *nedrog* or "those that are walking towards the *ne*" or holy place, and often a relationship based on human and divine participation will build up between the *nedrog* during their trip. The *khora* of the sacred place is a powerful method of raising one's level of consciousness. The *chak*, or prostration, induce a mental state of devotion and receptivity to the divine so that the offering is at once both donation and thanks.

Besides being a destination of pilgrimage, the sacred mountains are also objects of popular religious cults expressed with large festivals throughout the agricultural and pastoral calendars. Some of these events include horse races and archery and dance competitions. The contests are strictly for prestige and the honour of the individual and the community.

212-213 Festivities in honour of Gesar are about to start at Litang in Kham and the people are getting ready. The large white and blue tents being raised will house actors and spectators throughout the celebrations.

213 At Gesar festivals, the archery competition is one of the most important events; naturally, the archers are on horseback. The bows are prepared with care before the competition but even if their value is purely symbolic, only men are allowed to touch them.

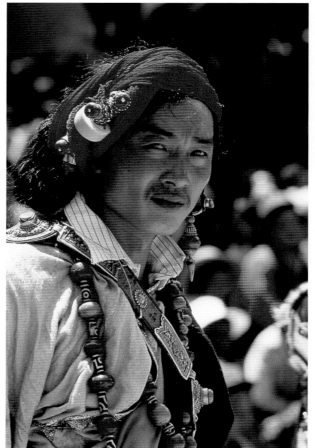

The large gatherings that used to bring horsemen from distant villages came to an end in 1959 but festivals of this type are still celebrated in much reduced and modified style.

The crowd watches attentively. Silk clothes and jewels make the usually tired-looking women seem much younger whilst the usually dirty and rough men seem almost elegant in their best, cleaned and mended chupa. *Farmers and nomads have come from all over and camped in white tents with blue embroidery for the harvest festival in the middle of the summer. The horse race, the most long-awaited event, is about to start and a shout rings out when the jockeys appear. Strong, massive, their saddles covered with fine cloth and harnesses adorned with coloured feathers, the horses shoot off in a cloud of dust and earth. At last the competitors reach the finish line, a coloured arch over which a bright red flag flutters, while the loudspeakers blare modern Tibetan songs. Even in the guise of the "Festival of Unity" (which was actually the origin of the festival, according to some local cadres) the horse race remains one of the people's favourite events, a ritual that has been repeated for centuries and which is spoken of in the epic poem of Gesar of Ling, the great hero.*

The son of a mountain deity and a demoness of the waters and the great hero of Tibetan epic literature, Gesar was also the author of astonishing and mighty deeds. The origin of his myth is lost in time but it resounds with the echo of distant civilizations which may have been brought with the hordes of wandering horsemen or caravans of foreign merchants. It speaks of grand cities, lovely palaces, heroic gestures and a certain Caesar or Kaiser that reigned at Krom... . A huge literature has been created around Gesar, conferences are held, and different trends of opinion are born. In the hinterlands of remote Tibet, however, occasionally one may hear an old and increasingly rare bard or minstrel singing the epic, sometimes accompanying himself on the *tamyen*, the typical Tibetan guitar.

A profound difference exists between the ancient concept of the mountain as god and the mountain as a destination of pilgrimage. In the first case, the mountain is a subject — it is part of a living world, the abode of the god and a god itself. In the second case, it is an object — a setting, a ritual instrument to be used on the path to spiritual liberation. The gods of the land did not lose their role when Buddhism arrived but were entered into the reality of the "things of the world" that need to be transcended. The two conceptions were integrated and overlaid so

214 top A young khampa is ready in his multi-coloured costume, concentrating on what is about to happen. For both those involved and the spectators, the tension is very high.

214-215 After three ritual turns by the horses around the incense brazier, the trials can begin. These are tests of speed but also ability and dexterity in which the rider must show uncommon skill. One of the most admired tests is to pick up a katak from the ground while at the gallop. A prize, for example a packet of cigarettes, is hidden inside.

215 top The athletes have prepared for months and now the competitors can finally show their skills in the ring of spectators. They ride with strength and elegance matching their movements to the fluidity of their powerful horses. Riding is an art that nomads learn from a young age and practise all their lives.

215 bottom There is a rest period at the end of a cycle of competitions for the men and animals to get their breath back. There is time to smoke a cigarette, drink a bowl of chang and swap notes and comments.

216 *The custom in Kham is that women wear their long black hair in thin plaits for the festival. They wear highly visible ornaments over their clothes, one of which is amber that, when plaited into the hair with coral, means that this is a girl of marriageable age.*

that the "mountain god of the land" also became a "mountain ritual instrument". That has been evident in Buddhist praxis since the times of the Tibetan kings.

It is also possible to find representatives of the cults of mountain deities in peripheral areas under the guise of Buddhist and Bonpo priests. One of them is the Aya. The anthropologist Charles Ramble notes that these are "mentioned in a number of Buddhist and Bonpo works ... it refers to a category of priests that is often associated with Shang Shung, ... they celebrate propitiatory rituals for local territorial divinities". Their sacral role is handed down "through the bones", i.e. from father to son. Picturesque figures in their multi-coloured ritual dress, the Aya are also "rain wizards" often found in other guises.

The clouds have massed and a storm is about to break. The smell of wet dust begins to rise from the ground. Please

don't let it be hail!!! In the monastery the abbot is sitting in front of a statue of Buddha meditating on the word of the Master commentated by Tsongkhapa. He is shaken by a sudden roll of thunder. Without thinking twice, he rises, takes some ritual objects and goes up to the roof. The clouds are dark and to the east they are edged with a murky white in a clear warning of hail. Almost standing straight up on his toes, he raises his hand, pushing the sacred object towards the sky. He gesticulates, shouts and spits in the direction of the clouds as the violent rain lashes against him. Uncaring, he repeats the action three times while the storm rages and all around the heights are covered with a white sheet, then ... one hundred yards from the village, the hail suddenly stops. "I can do it because I have the bones of the Aya" the abbot smiles, almost as if to excuse himself.

Hidden in the folds of Tibetan society, and occasionally only just tolerated, the oracles are even

216-217 At the end of the day, the people dance the shabdro once more. For the occasion, the women wear their best clothes, i.e. their elaborate traditional costumes. Silk brocade, large silver studs and rows of coral woven into elaborate hairstyles create an overall appearance that shows they come from a good family.

217 A row of women prepares for the dance. The rhythm is created by poignant songs marked by the clapping of hands and singing of the chorus by the spectators. A cup of chang between songs keeps the strength up allowing the dances to go on till late at night.

217

more difficult to find. They are usually women whose role it is to act as a medium for the voice of the mountain deity. They have few ritual objects left to them, most have gone missing or were destroyed or stolen during the Cultural Revolution, but they have enough to contact the deity. Women oracles in particular are considered enigmatic figures. A depository of popular wisdom and an expert in herbal medicines and psychology, she cures people in mind and body.

Her skills and capabilities are inherited and become apparent at a critical moment of her life. One oracle, a sheep farmer, tells the following story about the origin of her powers:

"I used to cure my family's sheep when I began to notice the presence of invisible spirits around me. I fell ill for a long time and only found relief when I attended religious ceremonies. A lama opened the channels for me and since then the god has been able to possess me. I have fallen into a trance many times, to help. People come to me when they have to make a choice". This oracle foresaw the arrival of the Red Guards and the destruction of her village in time for its inhabitants to escape.

Until a few decades ago, whenever the woman-oracle became aware of the onset of direct contact with the god, she would go to a grand lama who confirmed her ability and guided her actions. This arrangement enabled Buddhist institutions to keep this dark side of religion under control and to integrate it. Then came the Cultural Revolution when both male and female oracles were persecuted but in the early 1980s attitudes changed and they were legally "decriminalized"

although their activities remained branded as superstition. Many oracles took up their function again attended by young apprentices but as the lamas had now disappeared, they were approved instead by popular consent. Often oracles are people that otherwise lead a normal existence: they hoe the fields, graze their herds or work on the roads but, when it is necessary, the god speaks through them...

The woman-oracle is 67 years old and lives in a typical Tibetan farmhouse in a fertile valley. The setting is filled with ruins that seem to indicate an ancient caravan stop. When we arrived, the woman-oracle was not there as she had gone to celebrate some ceremonies in a nearby village. As soon as she crossed the threshold, the house filled with her strong and

218 top The festival in honour of Gesar also includes scenes of war, banditry and forays in which the hero always ends up triumphant. The actors wear brightly coloured and exaggerated clothes.

218 bottom In this image appeares a monk wearing a colorful costume for the show on Gesar's life. There are many characters in the representation of the adventures of the demi-god on earth.

218-219 *The actors are dressed and ready. Everyone knows the story and its variants and are proud to play the part of the hero and his companions. Gesar of Ling was the son of a mountain deity and a goddess of the waters; he was the redeemer that became man in order to free the country from the forces of evil.*

219 bottom *Traditional clothes of ancient Tibetan aristocracy, such as the hat shown in the photograph, are still used in the choreography of the epic.*

220 top left Aya, or Ala, priests are the living representatives of a tradition that goes back over a thousand years to the era of the Tibetan kings and pre-Buddhist religion. Their knowledge is handed down orally and their position is passed on "through the bones", i.e. from father to son.

220 top right Another form of religion about which little is known is that of the oracles, especially the women-oracles through whom the mountain deities speak. Persecuted during the Cultural Revolution but later rehabilitated though left without their ritual tools, they perform their rituals in the privacy of their homes. The photograph shows an oracle in a trance as the mountain deity Targo speaks through her.

220 bottom The mountain deity, Targo, is the lord of the elements and the owner of wild horses. He rules over the centre of the Chang Thang and is prayed to by both Bonpo and Buddhist pilgrims.

charismatic presence mixed with a streak of sweetness that quickly wins the visitor over. She speaks in a dialect that is difficult to understand but there is no difficulty in comprehension when we speak to her of the gods. Accompanying us is the son-in-law of the mayor who suffers from some troble and wishes to consult her. After numerous cups of butter tea in the smoky half-light of her kitchen, the woman invites us to watch the trance session. We follow her into the altar room, a simple place decorated with creased, modern holy prints. The sacred objects that are necessary in such circumstances are missing. She has only been left the highly polished mirror that reflects the clear light of the butter-lamps placed on the altar. She looks into the mirror placed in a bowl filled with barley grains and waits to recognize the gods that will possess her. After a long silence the woman presents her ritual offerings and begins to sing as her whole body begins to convulse. Suddenly her voice changes to the deep and melodious voice of her spirit guide, Sichun the yellow horseman, who asks her to

"be quick because his horse is waiting for him". When consulted, he rapidly offers diagnoses and therapy for the mayor's son-in-law. Then we offer him a katak which we put on the shoulders of the woman and he fades away. The god who replaces Sichun is Targo, the great mountain lord of the Tibetan lands in the north, the ancient kingdom of Shang Shung, protector of wild horses and nomads, Bonpo and Buddhist god together. In a deep voice he presents himself as a white-haired old man of great experience, then with a solemn voice he utters his response:

"Mi drupa midu, Pökyi shitsa sim go",
there is nothing that cannot be done,
you must hold firm to the roots of Tibet.

220-221 In the dyad of the mountain and lake, Lake Dangra Yumtsho in the picture is the female element. Like all divinities associated with natural elements, the lake goddess has different appearances. It is said that her beneficent form exists in the waters in a "castle suffused with turquoise light" whereas her terrifying counterpart dwells in the body of a black serpent. The lake's sacred shores are dotted with the many ruins of one of the capitals of the kingdom of Shang Shung.

221 bottom The gods that compose the dyad of the Chang Thang are also venerated in their terrifying aspect by the local communities.
These are their masks, red for Targo and blue for Dangra Yumtsho, which are kept in a small monastery on the lake shore.

224 The white katak, sign of favourable auspice, are hung on the big door leading inside the Potala palace.

Bibliography

Aziz, B.N. (1978) *Tibetan Frontier Families*. New Delhi: Vikas.

Bachelor, S. (1987) *The Tibet Guide*. London: Wisdom Publication.

Bacot, J., Thomas, F.W., Toussaint, CH. (1940) *Documents de Touen-Houang relatifs à l'histoire du Tibet*. Paris: Librairie orientaliste Paul Geuthner.

Barnett, R. (1996) *Cutting off the Serpent's Head: Policy Changes in Tibet, 1994-95"*. London/New York: Tibet Information Network.

Barnett, R. (1998) *A Poisoned Arrow — the Secret Petition of the 10th Panchen Lama*. London/New York: Tibet Information Network.

Barnett, R. (1998) "Lhasa la ville illisible" in *Tibètains, 1959-1999: 40 Ans de Colonisation*. Buffetrille K. & Ramble C. (Eds.) Paris: Editions Autrement.

Bellezza J.V. Divine Dyads (1997) *Ancient Civilisation in Tibet*. Dharamsala: Library of Tibetan Works and Archives.

Blondeau, A.M. (1998) *Tibetan Mountain Deities, Their Cults and Representations*. Vienna: Verlag der österreichischen Akademie der Wissenschaften.

Chayet A. (1994) *Art et Archéologie du Tibet*. Paris: Picard Editeur.

Chan, V. (1994) *Tibet Handbook*. Chico, California: Moon Publications.

Dalai Lama (1988) *La mia terra la mia gente*. Milano: Sperling & Kupfer Editori.

Dalai Lama (1995) *La via del Buddhismo tibetano*. Milano: Mondadori.

David Neel, A. (1992) *Viaggio di una parigina a Lhasa*. Roma: Biblioteca del Vascello.

Diemberger, H & Pasang Wangdu & Korfield M. & Jahoda C (1997) *Feast of Miracles*. Clusone: Porong Pema Chöding Editions.

Dowman K. (1988) *The Power-Places of Central Tibet, the Pilgrim's Guide*. London: Routhledge & P. Kegan

Garzanti, E. (1989) "La storia dell'India e la formazione dell'Himalaya" in *Le Scienze*.

Goldstein, M. (1989) *A History of Modern Tibet, 1913-1951*. University of California Press.

Goldstein, M & Beall, C. (1990) *Nomads of Western Tibet*. Hong Kong: Odyssey.

Howard-Bury, C. & Mallory G.L. (1991) *Everest Reconnaissance*. London: Hodder & Stougton.

Karmay, S.G. (1998) *The Arrow and the Spindle*. Kathmandu: Mandala Book Point.

Lhalungpa, L.P. (1979) *The Life of Milarepa*. London: Granada Publishing.

Li, F.K. & Coblin, W. S. (1987) *A Study of the Old Tibetan Incriptions*. Taipei: Institute of History and Philology Academia Sinica.

Mcdonald, A.W. (1997) *Mandala and Landscape*. New Delhi: D.K. Printworld.

Maraini, F. (1984) *Segreto Tibet*. dall'Oglio Milano.

Nebesky Wojkowitz, R. (1975) *Oracles and Demons of Tibet*. Graz: Akademische Druck u. Verlaganstalt.

Ngag dbang skal ldan egya mtsho (1996) *Shel dkar chos 'byung*. Translated by Pasang Wangdu and Hildegard Diemberger. Vienna: Verlag der österreichiscen Akademie der Wissenschaften.

Pasang Wangdu (1996) "Notes on a Chinese inscription of the Tang dinasty".*In Tibetan Studies Chinese Edition, nr.3*.

Pasang Wangdu & Diemberger H. (in stampa) *dBa' bzhed*. Translation and facsimile. Vienna: Verlag der österreichischen Akademie der Wissenschaften.

Petech. L. (1990) *Central Tibet and the Mongols*. Roma: IsMEO.

Ramble, C. (in print) "The *A-ya*: preliminary remarks on a category of priests in Tibet and Nepal". Acts of the 7th IATS Congress, Bloomington, July 1998.

Richardson, H. & Snellgrove, D. (1987) *Cultural History of Tibet*. Boston: Shambala.

Schaller, G. (1997) *Tibet's Hidden Wilderness*. New York: Harry N. Abrams.

Schuh, D. (1988) *Das Archiv des Klosters bKra-sis-bsam-gtan-glin von sKid-gron*. Bonn: WGH Wissenschafts Verlag GmbH.

Sironi M.A. & Diemberger H. (1995) *La Storia del Cristallo Bianco*. Clusone: Ferrari Editrice.

Snellgrove, D. (1987) *Indo-Tibetan Buddhism*. Boston: Shambala.

Stein, R. (1986) *La civiltà tibetana*. Torino: Einaudi.

Taylor C. (1995) *Tibet*. Torino: Lonely Planet, Guide E.D.T.

Tucci, G. (1980) *A Lhasa e oltre*. Roma: New Compton editori.

Tucci, G. (1976) *Le religioni del Tibet*. Rona: Edizioni Mediterranee.

Uray, G. (1972) "Queen Sad-mar-kar's Songs in the Old Tibetan Chronicle" in *Acta Orientalia*, tomus XXV, p. 5-38.

Wang Yao, (1994) "Hu Yaobang's Visit to Tibet, May 22-31, 1980" in: Barnett, R. & Akiner, S. *Resistance and Reform in Tibet*. London: Hurst & Company.

Illustration credits

Archivio White Star: pages 30, 31, 32, 33, 34 top, 40-41, 42 top, 44, 45, 46, 47, 49 bottom, 56 bottom, 57.

Marcello Bertinetti/Archivio White Star: pages 1, 4-5, 6-7, 8 left, 8 bottom, 9 bottom, 14-15, 20 top and bottom, 20-21, 21 top, 27 left top, 27 bottom left, 62 left bottom, 66 top, 68 top, 72, 73, 76 top, 78 top, 79, 83 top, 86, 87, 88 top and bottom, 88-89, 89 bottom, 92, 93, 96 top, 98, 99 top and centre, 101 top, 108, 109, 110, 111, 112, 112-113, 113 bottom, 119 top, 123 bottom right, 126, 127, 128, 129, 136-137, 137 centre and bottom, 138, 139, 140, 141, 142, 143, 144-145, 146 centre and bottom, 146-147, 147, 148, 149, 150 right top, 151 bottom, 152 bottom, 153 top and bottom, 156, 157, 163 bottom, 164-165, 168 top left, 170 left, 171 top, 172, 173, 174, 175 bottom, 176, 177, 178, 179, 182, 183, 184, 185, 186 top and bottom, 186-187, 187 top, 188, 189 bottom, 191 top right, 191 centre and bottom, 198, 202, 203, 206 bottom, 208 top and centre, 208-209, 209 top, 211 top right and left, 224.

John Ackerly/Tibet Images: page 67 top.

Anders Andersen/Tibet Images: pages 63 left bottom, 99 bottom left, 137 top.

Associated Press: pages 66 bottom, 61 centre.

Tiziana and Gianni Baldizzone: pages 10-11, 12-13, 20 centre, 22-23, 64-65, 76 bottom, 76-77, 80, 80-81, 81 top, 84, 84-85, 85 bottom, 90 bottom, 94-95, 96 bottom, 96-97, 101 bottom, 114, 115, 116, 117, 119 bottom, 120, 121, 122, 123 left bottom, 132, 133, 134-135, 162 top, 162-163, 168 bottom, 194, 195, 196, 197, 207 bottom, 208 bottom, 212, 213, 214, 215, 216, 217, 218, 219.

Robin Bath/Tibet Images: page 167 bottom.

Bibliothèque Nationale de France,

Paris: pages 24 centre left, 35 bottom.

The British Library: pages 36-37 bottom.

Franc Charton: pages 90 top, 146 top, 168-169, 204 top and bottom.

Ian Cumming/Tibet Images: pages 2-3, 62-63, 68-69, 101 centre, 158 top and centre, 158-159, 159 bottom, 166-167, 180, 181 bottom.

Nick Dawson/Tibet Images: page 145 bottom.

Department of Information & International Relations/ Tibet Images: pages 61 bottom, 59 bottom.

Hildegard Diemberger: pages 24 left bottom, 27 centre, 69 bottom, 85 top, 164, 207 top and centre, 220, 220-221, 221 bottom.

Kurt Diemberger/Leicaflex: pages 14 bottom, 15 bottom, 24 top, 130-131, 200 left top, 200 left bottom, 200 bottom.

Maria Antonia Sironi Diemberger: pages 67 bottom left, 125 bottom, 165 bottom.

Joel Ducange/Agence Top: page 170 bottom.

E.T. Archive: pages 29 top, 161 bottom.

Mary Evans Picture Library: pages 34-35.

Fondazione Alexandra David-Néel, Digne les Bains: page 49 top.

Didier Givois: pages 82-83.

Gino Gomba: pages 26 bottom, 83 bottom, 90 centre, 91 bottom.

Philippe Guignard/Hemispheres: pages 65 top.

Heinrich Harrer: pages 27 bottom right, 48 centre and bottom, 50, 51, 52, 53, 58 centre and bottom, 59 right top, 60 top, 62 right bottom, 65 top right.

Guntram Hazod: page 144 bottom.

The Illustrated London News Picture Library: pagg 54, 55, 58 top, 61 top.

Thomas L. Kelly: pages 16 top and bottom, 17 top, 28 top, 29 left centre, 36-37 top, 43 centre right, 61 centre, 74-75, 76 centre, 77 top, 160, 161 centre, 166 top right and bottom.

Earl Kowall: pages 66-67.

Irene Kristalis/Tibet Images: page 200 top.

Charles Lenars: pages 25, 29 right bottom, 36 top, 150 bottom, 150 left top, 150-151, 154 centre and bottom.

Manuel Lugli: page 103 top and bottom.

Kay Maeritz: page 166 top left.

Foto Mairani: page 15 top.

Carlo Meazza: pages 106 centre, 113 top, 124 bottom, 124-125, 125 top, 210, 211 bottom right.

John Miles/Tibet Images: page 63 right bottom.

Colin Monteath/Hedgehog House: pages 16-17, 17 bottom, 78-79, 100 top, 100-101, 102 top, 104-105, 154 top left, 190, 191 top left, 206 left.

Colin Monteath/Mountain Camera: page 103 centre.

Pat Morrow: pages 8-9, 97 bottom, 106 top, 106 bottom, 106-107, 122-123, 136 bottom, 192, 193, 204 centre, 206-207.

NASA: pages 18-19, 19, 70, 71.

National Palace Museum, Taipei/ The Bridgeman Art Library: page 28 bottom.

Ernesto Noriega/Tibet Images: page 155 bottom.

Ernani Orcorte/Realy Easy Star: pages 63 centre right, 152-153.

Photobank: pages 65 bottom, 107 left bottom, 158 bottom, 174-175, 188-189.

Private Collection/The Bridgeman Art Library: page 24 right bottom.

Hugh Richardson/Trustees of The British Museum/Tibet Images: page 63 top.

Galen Rowell/Franca Speranza: pages 118 top and bottom, 199, 201, 205 bottom.

Galen Rowell/Mountain Light: pages 26-27, 63 left centre, 82 bottom, 90-91, 118-119, 145 top, 180-181, 204-205.

Royal Geographical Society: pages 38-39, 39 bottom, 42 bottom, 43 top left, 43 bottom left and right, 43 top right, 56-57, 64 top, 65 centre right.

Gerar Sioen/Regina M. Anzenberger: page 161 top.

Paul Slattery/Tibet Images: page 81 bottom.

Sean M. Smith/Tibet Images: pages 102-103.

Sotheby's Picture Library: page 34 bottom.

F.Spencer-Chapman/Pitt Rivers Museum/Tibet Images: pages 48-49.

N.Tapsell/FFotograff: pages 63 top right, 162 centre and bottom, 186 centre.

Mike Tibbets/Tibet Images: page 88 centre.

Tibet Images: pages 59 left top, 60 bottom, 67 bottom right, 211 bottom left.

Angelo Tondini/Focus team: pages 170-171, 171 bottom.

Yeo Dong Wan/Tibet Images: page 68 bottom.

Alison Wright: pages 107 bottom right, 154-155, 168 top right, 169 bottom.